SUNNY-SIDE UP

SUNNY-SIDE UP

MORE THAN 100 BREAKFAST & BRUNCH RECIPES

FROM *the Essential Egg* **TO** *the Perfect Pastry*

WAYLYNN LUCAS

RODALE

NEW YORK

Published in the United States by Rodale Books, an imprint of the
Crown Publishing Group, a division of Penguin Random House LLC,
New York.
crownpublishing.com
rodalebooks.com

RODALE and the Plant colophon are registered trademarks of
Penguin Random House LLC.

Library of Congress Cataloging-in-Publication Data is available
upon request.

ISBN 978-1-63565-370-0
Ebook ISBN 978-1-63565-371-7

Printed in China

Book and cover design by Sonia Persad
Cover photographs by Aubrie Pick

10 9 8 7 6 5 4 3 2 1

First Edition

This book is dedicated to my mom, whose endless support and brutal honesty toward my food has pushed me and allowed me to achieve my dreams.

To all those I have worked with over the years who taught and showed me new ways to approach food to discover what I am truly capable of.

To God for making it all possible and filling my heart with love to see my true passion in life and for giving me the strength to never stop chasing my dreams, and to keep creating new ones.

Lastly, to all the meals, people, and experiences I have had in my life that inspired this book.

CONTENTS

WAY WITH EGGS

So many chefs have a thing with eggs. The egg is not just the basis of breakfast or baking—it's the basis of life itself. When you hold one in your hand, you can't help but want to protect it, and yet you try to break it by squeezing it. It's stronger than it looks. I admit, I, too, really have a thing for eggs. They still surprise me and fascinate me after all these years in the kitchen. But one thing I know for certain about cooking eggs is that the secret to making them obsession-worthy is all in the handling. And that same handling is also the secret technique to successful cooking, baking . . . even relationships!

The famous chef Auguste Escoffier said that of all the ingredients used in cooking, "not one is so fruitful of variety, so universally liked, and so complete in itself as an egg." In other words, the egg is like the friend everyone loves. Whip it (although I wouldn't suggest you do that to a friend) and you get meringue. Fold it into batter and make your cake fluffier and airier. Temper it into cream sauces and soups and magically make them thicker and silkier. Froth it and make a killer cocktail topping. Fry it sunny-side up and let it ooze onto buttered toast for a decadent feast that'll run you about seventy-five cents.

The unwritten (well, until now) rule is that how well you can cook an egg is a testament to how well you can cook. Chef Jacques Pépin (who has written twenty-six cookbooks, won multiple James Beard awards, and helmed several successful cooking shows) once said that he judges a chef by the way they make an omelet. His former costar on the show *Cooking at Home,* none other than Julia Child, described how her Cordon Bleu cooking instructor Max Bugnard used the "humble scrambled egg" as a lesson that "one pay attention, learn the correct technique, and that one enjoy one's cooking." So for me, the simple act of scrambling an egg is the foundation of all cooking and baking techniques.

As I began to think about my cookbook, recipes for the far-out creative stuff I'm known for ran through my mind—fun pastries and desserts and crazy combinations like my Lemon Meringue Pie with Pop Rocks—but what I could not keep from taking over my cookbook brain was **EGGS**! Eggs in burritos. Eggs sandwiched between two waffles. Egg stratas and frittatas! Eggs scrambled on the stove and eaten standing up in the kitchen. And, of course, eggs sunny-side up! So what better way to celebrate the egg than with a breakfast cookbook?

But just in case you thought we were only cooking eggs, this cookbook also includes my favorite recipes for healthy powerhouses like smoothies, homemade yogurt, superfood bowls, oatmeal, and breakfast bars, as well as savory biscuits and breads and even cocktails for a little day drinking. One of the main reasons I love breakfast and brunch so much is that it's the one meal where you can **EAT DESSERT AS YOUR WHOLE MEAL!** Muffins, French toast, pancakes, waffles, and cinnamon rolls aren't just an **OPTIONAL** dessert when you eat them for breakfast. They **ARE** the meal! Think about it: at what other meal can you enjoy a flaky buttery croissant oozing with chocolate **AND** have a scrambled egg on the side? This is why I love you, breakfast. And this is why I must share your charms with the world.

Eggs plus baking plus baking with eggs— as a pastry chef and breakfast fanatic, it all just gets me beyond excited. In this book you'll find super-easy recipes, recipes you can grab on the go or sip by the bar, and even a few superstar baking recipes that will turn you into a breakfast-baking and -cooking pro. I wanted to create a cookbook that wasn't intimidating and wasn't just for show. I wanted a cookbook for everyone, with straightforward simple ingredients you can find at your basic market, recipes that I love, and things that I want to do and eat everyday while putting my professional chef spin on things and giving some chef's tips along the way.

Don't stress over any of these recipes! I should know better than most that you don't need to be "born a chef" to become one. Believe it or not, my family used to tease me when I was growing up that I couldn't boil water to save my life. My mother is an amazing cook, and food was at the center of our family's daily life. At home, the Food Network was always on TV—I mean **ALWAYS** on the TV, morning, noon, and night. The old-school Food Network shows like *Two Fat Ladies, Barefoot Contessa,* and *Nigella,* just to name a few favorites. Going to restaurants was our version of family bonding. Vacations were planned around what meals we would eat and what restaurants we would visit. So I was immersed in the sumptuous world of food from an early age, but my aptitude for cooking was all but hidden.

There was one clue that I might make a good pastry chef, but at the time it presented itself only as an extremely irritating habit that drove my mother mad to watch. When I would eat my morning toast, I would spend five minutes evenly spreading the butter to all the edges, making sure no nook or cranny went unfilled. By the time I finished, the toast would be stone cold and my mother would be beyond annoyed at me. It wasn't until many years later that in hindsight I was able to see that glimmer of the future pastry chef I would become—it was that need in me, that little touch of OCD, that was not going to eat even a piece of toast without having it properly buttered for maximum eating enjoyment! Every bite needed to be perfect. I carry that mentality into my desserts today, and it hasn't failed me yet.

During the summers growing up, I always worked in restaurants. I worked every job, from dishwasher to busser to prep cook to hostess. I was in the world of food, but I had yet to find my place in it. I'd been led to believe working in the front-of-house positions was a step up from some of the menial work I'd done in the kitchen, but I found that working up front was not for me. I preferred the company of cooks and dishwashers to customers.

After a foray into the fashion industry, I moved to Costa Rica and fell in love with the little village where I was living. The only problem was, it needed a coffee shop. So I opened a coffee shop. At the same time, I started experimenting with recipes, and I loved the instant effect my baked goods had on people: they made people happy! So the coffee shop morphed into a bakery, I began creating all kinds of goodies to go with the coffee, and the happy little village was even happier with all the sweets I was churning out. Experiencing people's positive reaction to my muffins and scones gave me an instant buzz. The connection between food and happiness I'd experienced with my family had come right back to the center of my daily life. This time I was the one making the magic, and I was hooked!

From Costa Rica, I was off to culinary school to learn the science and techniques of cooking and pastry making. My previously annoying attention to detail when it came to buttering my toast was now an advantage. It was and is in my personality to think beyond just getting a recipe finished— I think, **HOW IS SOMEONE GOING TO ENJOY THIS? WHAT IS THE BEST WAY TO MAKE SURE THEY HAVE THE BEST EXPERIENCE EATING THIS?**

On *Cake Wars,* for example, if the layers of a cake aren't even or one layer has more frosting than another, you aren't getting the perfect bite every time. My attention to detail does not always pan out well for the contestants, but even those bakers who do not share my OCD tendencies do share a desire that's even more important: to create something that makes people happy.

Speaking of *Cake Wars,* it's hard to describe the joy I have for getting that job. After all those years of growing up with Food Network, it truly is a huge dream come true—beyond huge, actually, and in a weird way, I'm seeing my life come full circle. I'm beyond blessed and grateful and still have to pinch myself. My mom is still obsessed with Food Network, and knowing I'm part of it makes me so proud.

So it's been a journey to get to this point where I can share what I've learned, and I'm here to lead you through a baking and cooking adventure of your own that will have you making breakfast and brunch dishes, from eggs to fancy pastries, like a true chef.

As long as you are able to follow directions, you're halfway there. The second half of my equation is the technique or the finesse, **WHICH YOU ALSO DO NOT HAVE TO BE BORN WITH!** Finesse is simply the art of using a delicate hand—handling with care, in other words. You can cook and bake without finesse, and what you make will probably still be pretty good. But if you can start adding a little finesse, your savory dishes and baked goods are going to go from good to amazing pretty quickly, and you're going to love the process of getting better and better every time you make something as you're able to pay more and more attention to the little details that will make all the difference.

Making eggs is the perfect way to practice your touch, your finesse. Handle the eggs gently, taking your time, allowing the egg to be itself . . . the whole process is kinda sexy, if you think about it. Have a mind-set of love, not angst. Treat your eggs and your baking lovingly, caressingly, following what Chef Bugnard said: pay attention, use the correct technique, and enjoy the process. Give all your cooking and baking this kind of mindfulness and love, and you will be a rock star in the kitchen, I promise. You'll master scrambled eggs, biscuits, beignets, and beyond.

And that's really what this book is all about: giving your dishes—whether it's an egg sunny-side up, homemade Prosciutto-Gruyère Croissants (page 152), or simply a piece of thoroughly buttered toast—the same love and attention you'd give your best friend, your spouse, or your pet! When that's what you give, you'll be shocked and pleased by the yummy goodness you get back. What a great way to start (or finish) your day.

PREP TALK FOR A SUNNY KITCHEN

Remember my number one simple secret to successful breakfast and baking in general: treat it with love and attention and handle with care.

That being said . . . there are ways to make your experience more successful and more fun. For example, taking the time to properly measure out your ingredients and having them and your equipment ready and accounted for before you start is what chefs call *mise en place*. Do this! Also, please read through the entire recipe and instructions before you start, even if you do so super quick. Get an idea of what's ahead . . . you'll be glad you did. I hate doing this, too, but after enough mistakes, I've learned to just do it! The last thing you want is to be scrambling to find the baking soda while you're in the middle of mixing your batter or, worse, to forget an ingredient entirely. Trust me, it happens to even the best of us. Your mind wanders, you get overwhelmed, nervous, flustered, your kids are yelling at you, and before you know it, you've messed up your recipe. Try not to let this happen. The kitchen should be a sunny zone. Don't go to the dark side of chaos and angst.

If I told you how many cakes I've eaten on *Cake Wars* that were missing the sugar, oil, spices, baking powder, or other ingredients, you probably wouldn't believe me! Take my word for it: it's not fun and nobody ends up happy. The cake doesn't taste good, and the bakers feel like they wasted all that time and energy thanks to a forgotten teaspoon or two of some essential ingredient. So save yourself the anxiety and prepare your ingredients and equipment with care ahead of time. **MISE EN PLACE** is one of those professional chef "secrets" that is really, **REALLY** easy for even a newbie to do. Enjoy the experience and feeling of measuring and laying out your ingredients. You are setting yourself up for success, so you are already winning.

Take your time. Patience is a virtue in life and in baking. Certain things cannot and should not be rushed. The process of cooking and baking is just as magical and enjoyable as eating the finished product. It is its own journey, so enjoy it. What's that obnoxious but true saying you see everywhere? "It's not the destination, it's the journey"? Well, in our case, it definitely **IS** the tasty destination, but the journey is where the magic happens, and I am a true believer that you can undoubtedly taste the love that goes into any recipe.

I have few rules in my life, but one of them is "Never cook or bake in a bad mood." Lucky for me, cooking and baking can turn even my worst moods around, which is why I love it. If you are not a morning person, making breakfast could even be the key to starting your day in a better place. Play music, sing, dance, drink a mimosa, drink another mimosa, talk to yourself, pretend you are the host of your own cooking show . . . **HAVE FUN!**

Everything about food is an experience: shopping for it, preparing it, cooking it, eating it, going out to eat it, even remembering it. How you approach this experience is up to you—it could be with worry and hurry or it could be with care and love. Food has the ability to create the most impactful memories we have in our lives. A dish, a spice, a flavor, a smell can transport you to past places in your life in an instant. Food **IS** life. Food is fun, joy, happiness, and food is extremely intimate.

When I was a young cook just starting out, I worked for a very noteworthy chef who pulled me aside and explained the importance of what we were doing, to make sure I truly understood the gravity of it. He told me that every person who ate our food, every guest who came into the restaurant, was placing all their trust in us, that

we were creating something with our own two hands that eventually they would place in their mouths, into their bodies. There are few things more intimate than that. I will never forget his words or how humble they made me feel. Keeping them in mind has given me the utmost respect for everything about food and cooking and what I have been so fortunate to do as a career.

Now, to reiterate one of my most important points about cooking, don't be intimidated by this responsibility of creating something other people will be putting into their bodies. Simply handle the process with care. Give it your attention and love, and it will be received in the exact same way. Whisk, scramble, and serve with love, and you'll always be on the sunny side of the kitchen.

HELPFUL HARDWARE

There's not one piece of equipment that is *absolutely* essential on this list, so don't be sad if you're missing anything. I get it—kitchen gadgets aren't always cheap. But these are the tools I've found most helpful for creating my favorite breakfasts and brunches, so you might want to think about adding some of these to your kitchen wish list.

STURDY METAL WHISK
This is essential for whipping air into eggs, especially for perfect fluffy scrambled eggs and frittatas.

RUBBER SPATULA Heatproof is best, so if you leave it sitting in a hot pot or pan, it doesn't melt or burn your hand when you go to grab it.

FOOD PROCESSOR These can be expensive but are *sooo* key in the kitchen. They do it all—chop veggies, shred cheese, make pie and quiche dough, quickly mix sauces, purée things. You can even use it instead of a blender. This is one piece of hardware I highly recommend.

STAND MIXER with PADDLE, WHISK, and DOUGH HOOK ATTACHMENTS For bread making, a stand mixer is essential. I have made bread dough by hand, and trust me, it's not something you want to do. Making batter is so much faster and easier with a stand mixer. It's an investment, but a staple. I, of course, love my KitchenAid.

SILICONE BAKING MAT
This is the best solution when you're baking cookies or breads, anything where you'd otherwise have to use parchment paper to line a pan or something to grease it. I do not like wasting paper products when I don't have to, and I really do not like washing all that yucky grease off my baking sheets. You can wash and reuse a silicone baking mat for a lifetime as long as you take care of it, so don't scrub it with harsh sponges, and don't ever cut on it!

WAFFLE MAKER Can't make waffles without one. Good thing they sell 'em cheap.

ICE POP MOLDS You can get creative and make ice pops in plastic cups or other household items, but good molds make it fun, cute, and easy.

A GOOD BLENDER A good-quality high-speed blender will get the job done in half the time with half the effort and not leave you with chunks or lots of air bubbles. I love my Vitamix.

JUICER Juicing can be a pain. There's lots of cleanup. The juicers are kinda heavy. But it's so worth it— try it if you haven't. I love my Breville juicer.

OFFSET SPATULA This under-the-radar tool is great for spreading batter and for serving.

THREE GOOD KNIVES
Here's what you need: paring, bread (serrated), and chef's.

KITCHEN TIMER A kitchen timer is a must, as even the best chefs get distracted and forget to check their baking goodies. Time is crucial for a perfect baked good. Even one minute too long in the oven can make a big difference. I like to use a magnetic timer that I keep above the oven so it's right there. I always set my timer for just under half the total estimated bake time. This is when I will rotate the pan, then reset the timer for the rest of the bake time. During the last few minutes of baking, I will check the pan frequently. You can always keep baking, but you can't un-bake something.

DIGITAL THERMOMETER

Let's all be real: it's impossible to read those old-school thermometers. Digital is better. It's 2019. Make your life easy! I like the digital thermometers with the alarms so you can set the temp and it will alert you when ready.

A NOTE ON INGREDIENTS

I created this book to be easy, educational, and fun. So it was essential that all the ingredients needed would be things you can find at your regular ol' supermaket—no crazy specialty store necessary. As I was making and testing all my recipes, I did have to go to Whole Foods for a couple of things and order a few things from Amazon, as sometimes my small little mountain town of Park City, Utah, doesn't have all the creature comforts you might expect. With that in mind, know that you don't have to buy all organic ingredients if that's not your thing. Yes, I'm a firm believer in organic and every ingredient makes a difference in a recipe, but I am also frugal and realistic. If I am making a huge batch of something, I will probably buy the cheaper stuff, and if I am making a recipe for a special occasion, I might splurge. I always am mindful of my produce and meat—these are the areas where it does make a difference to me. Take the time to look through the fruits and veggies and pick the best, ripest ones.

SALT There are a lot of different salts out there, and they are not all created equal. Different salts can have different uses in the kitchen. I recommend using Baleine sea salt (I love La Baleine) or kosher salt. All the recipes in this book, unless otherwise noted, were tested using fine sea salt. My favorite fancy finishing salt for certain items is Maldon sea salt. It is made up of large, beautiful flakes and crystals of salt. This is what I use to finish off cookies and biscuits. Please note that depending on what type of salt you use, you may have to make some adjustments in the amount. Most of the pastry/baking recipes will be all right; however, on the savory dishes you may taste a difference. In the end, season to *your* taste. Remember, start small and add more as needed. You can't un-salt or un-season your food!

SUGAR Most of the time I use organic sugar. It is less refined and has a coarser grain, so it is not the best choice for *all* things. I will specify in the recipe if another type of sugar should be used. For example, organic sugar should not be used for meringues, or in any recipe in which you need the sugar to dissolve easily and perfectly. For brown sugar, I always prefer organic, even though it can be a little more expensive, because it has a richer, better taste. Make sure to seal any opened bag extra tight. I find organic brown sugar hardens faster than regular brown sugar.

YEAST Yeast comes in different forms. All the recipes in this book call for active dry yeast, which you can buy at any supermarket in a small jar or little packets. It does have a shelf life, so refrigerate after opening and pay attention to the expiration date. You cannot equally interchange dry yeast and fresh yeast. It's helpful to note that each ¼-ounce packet of active dry yeast contains approximately 2¼ teaspoons.

BUTTER Butter is butter, and you can use any unsalted butter for any recipe in this book. There are differences in taste and quality, though, so there are certain times when you may want to splurge on an expensive, high-quality butter—such as when making croissants, brioche, and biscuits—and those times won't be cheap, as those recipes are also butter-forward, so you'll be using a lot. I like Kerrygold when I'm splurging on fancy butter. Otherwise, I buy whatever unsalted butter is on sale at the market.

FLOUR I created the recipes in this book to only use all-purpose flour, with a few exceptions where I specifically call for whole wheat. I don't enjoy having to keep track of different kinds of flour in my pantry. For those who are still curious, however, there is pastry flour, the finest flour that helps make delicate pastries, all-purpose in the middle of the spectrum, and bread flour, which is the coarsest of the flours and is used for bread, as it provides the most gluten and creates the strongest structure for loaves.

EGGS Eggs are eggs are eggs. If you can get your hands on fresh eggs, that is always best! However, you cannot use fresh eggs to make meringue—eggs have to be store-bought to work for a meringue. The most important thing to be mindful of with eggs is the size. I use large eggs in all my recipes. Extra large is fine, too, but not small.

MILK When it comes to milk and baking, whole milk is the only way to go. This one can be hard for me, as I always like to cut out fat when I can, but you need that extra fat for moist, rich, delicious baked goods. The only time it's all right to substitute low-fat dairy would be when a recipe calls for yogurt. Low-fat yogurt—*not* fat-free, just low-fat—will still yield a yummy treat. But if you can, try to go full-fat . . . everything in moderation.

HIGH ALTITUDE BAKING

For high-altitude baking, raise the oven temperature by 25 degrees and lessen the amount of leavening agent used.

EGG OBSESSIONS

& OTHER SAVORIES

MELT-IN-YOUR-MOUTH SCRAMBLED EGGS

If you use no other recipe in this book, you're going to thank me for this one. It's not long because it's complicated—it's long because it gives some detail on the care and handling of the eggs, that secret technique that will really make the difference between good eggs and melt-in-your-mouth eggs. If you bomb the first time, keep trying. Eggs come by the dozen, so don't be afraid to start over.

4 large eggs

2 tablespoons whole milk or half-and-half

¼ teaspoon fine sea salt

1 tablespoon unsalted butter

1 wedge the Laughing Cow Light Creamy Swiss Cheese, broken into pieces (see Note; optional)

1 Crack the eggs into a medium bowl. Using a whisk, vigorously beat the eggs until you see bubbles and the eggs get super frothy. The key here is to incorporate air in order to give you fluffy eggs, so beat away. Add the milk and salt, then whisk again until combined.

2 Heat a large nonstick skillet over medium heat. Once the skillet is warm, add the butter. As it melts, lift and rotate the pan to coat the entire skillet with butter, being extra sure to cover the sides and inside edge—this is extremely important. The edge of the skillet is where the eggs will be the thinnest, thus where the eggs will cook the quickest, so you want to make sure it is well coated with butter so the eggs don't stick. Be careful not to brown the butter or allow the skillet to get too hot. When the skillet is hot and coated with butter, pour in the egg mixture. Add the cheese (if using).

3 Reduce the heat to medium-low. Once you notice the eggs starting to thicken and cook through, which will most likely be right away, use a rubber spatula to gently scrape a line through the eggs from the top of the skillet to the bottom and then again from left to right, making a "plus sign." Run your spatula around the outer edge of the skillet, drawing a circle, to pull in the outer edge of the eggs and allow the uncooked liquid eggs to fill in the spaces you just cleared with your spatula. Let the eggs cook, undisturbed, for a minute or two,

NOTE   My secret weapon for extra-creamy cheesy eggs is to add a wedge of the Laughing Cow Light Creamy Swiss Cheese. I add 1 triangle of the cheese per 3 or 4 eggs. Break the cheese into pieces and add it to the eggs as directed in the recipe.

MOOOVE OVER, MAYO

The Laughing Cow Light Creamy Swiss Cheese isn't just my secret weapon for killer eggs—it's also my healthy replacement for mayo and cheese in sandwiches. It's creamy and cheesy, so it does the job of both mayo and cheese in a sandwich while cutting the calories way down. No, I am not a paid sponsor—I just lived off the stuff as a young teenager backpacking in Europe, and it's been one of my favorite staples ever since. It's cheap, too. Spread it all over a plain baguette and you're good to go.

WHY WHISK?

A whisk is a crucial kitchen tool for a lot of recipes—especially for scrambled eggs, as the sole purpose and design of a whisk is to incorporate air. All the wires on a whisk allow air to be incorporated and air bubbles to form, resulting in a fluffier, lighter finished product that you just can't achieve with a regular spoon or even a fork. Also, a plastic or rubber whisk just won't get the job done. Go with metal, always.

then *slowly* use your spatula to swirl the eggs around the skillet in large movements, allowing the uncooked egg to make contact with the skillet and moving the cooked parts out of the way. The most important things to remember are to not overmix the eggs and to treat them gently. You are looking for fluffy, melt-in-your-mouth scrambled eggs. You can even pick up the skillet to swirl the uncooked eggs around to make contact with the skillet, always gently scraping the outer edge of the skillet and eggs toward the inside. You don't want the outside edge to get too thin or cook too long—if it is too thin on the edge, you get those strange, plastic-looking sheets of egg. I'm sure you have seen those before—they're most unenjoyable to eat and not pretty on a plate, either.

4   Let the eggs cook and come together in large pieces. As you finish cooking the eggs, gently moving your spatula around the skillet and through the eggs, they will break up on their own. You can gently flip sections of the egg over, almost like gently folding whipped cream into melted chocolate for a mousse or a meringue into your dry ingredients for a cake, to cook them thoroughly. Cook the eggs until they have set and come together and there is no more liquid in the skillet, but they are still moist and shiny and wet looking.

5   This is important: remove the skillet from the heat when the eggs are still wet looking, just before they are cooked all the way through, as they will continue to cook in the residual heat of the hot skillet and the eggs themselves.

6   Before serving, quickly stir the eggs around the skillet and then immediately divide them between two plates. Serve and enjoy!

CRACK IT LIKE A CHEF

Always crack your eggs on a flat surface. When you crack them on the edge of the counter or the rim of a bowl, the shell cracks into the egg, and you're more likely to end up with little broken pieces mixed in with your egg. Also, remember to be gentle. It doesn't take much force to break an eggshell. I crack my eggs into a small bowl first and then add them to the skillet or bowl. It's a lot easier to pick out any eggshells from the small bowl of just eggs than from a skillet of potatoes or a bowl of batter.

EGGS SUNNY-SIDE UP

If, the first time you try these, the yolk gets too firm for your taste or the white doesn't cook all the way through, don't worry. They'll still taste good. And if they don't, just try again. Or stick them between two pieces of toast slathered in butter with a slice of your favorite cheese—I like Laughing Cow or sharp Cheddar—and you'll be just fine.

½ tablespoon unsalted butter

2 large eggs

Pinch of fine sea salt

Dash of freshly ground black pepper

1   In a small nonstick skillet over medium heat, melt the butter. When it is just barely starting to bubble, carefully crack the eggs into the skillet, being careful not to break the yolk or get eggshell in the skillet.

2   Sprinkle the eggs with the salt and pepper. Cook, undisturbed, for about 30 seconds, or until the bottoms of the eggs are white and starting to set. Working one at a time, with the tip of the spatula, where the white is the thickest (usually next to the yolk), break into it and gently pull it back. Allow the clear uncooked white to pool into the pan to cook. The idea here is to get the thick, clear, uncooked egg white into contact with the skillet. Do this a few times in the thickest areas.

3   Place a lid on the skillet and reduce the heat to low. Cook for a minute or two, until the whites are no longer clear but the yolks are still unbroken and runny. If you prefer a firmer yolk, simply cook the eggs a little longer. Uncover and remove from the heat as soon as it is cooked to your liking. (Leaving the lid on will allow the eggs to keep cooking.)

BACON, TOMATO, AND CHEDDAR BREAD PUDDING (BREAKFAST STRATA)

Bread pudding, you rock my world. Custard-soaked bread baked and served crunchy on top—yum! This is my savory version of a very smart invention. Breakfast bread puddings are sometimes called strata. Technically, this is not a strata—*strata* means "layers" in Italian, and in a true strata you would layer the bread with filling and repeat. But who needs to get so technical? Whatever you want to call it, it's delicious.

9 large eggs

2½ cups whole milk

½ cup heavy cream

½ teaspoon fine sea salt

¼ teaspoon freshly ground black pepper

¼ teaspoon fresh thyme leaves

1¾ cups shredded aged white Cheddar

10 to 11 cups (1-inch-pieces) stale bread (I like challah or brioche)

20 slices bacon

1½ cups grape or cherry tomatoes, halved

1 Preheat the oven to 375°F. Lightly grease a 9 by 11-inch baking dish—the deeper the better. (I use an oval baking dish that is approximately 9 by 11 by 2½ inches, which is deeper than the typical rectangular baking dish. Don't stress it, though—you might just have to omit a little of the mixture if it won't all fit.)

2 In a large bowl, whisk the eggs. Stir in the milk, cream, salt, pepper, thyme, and 1¼ cups of the cheese and set aside.

3 Place the bread pieces in an extra-large bowl and set aside.

4 In a large skillet, cook the bacon until almost fully cooked, about 10 minutes (the bacon will finish cooking in the oven, and if you fully cook the bacon before adding it, it will lose some of its flavor). Transfer the bacon to a plate to cool. Spoon 3 tablespoons of the bacon grease from the skillet into the milk mixture and stir to combine.

recipe continues

5 Chop the cooled bacon. Add the bacon and tomatoes to the bread. Pour the milk mixture over the bread mixture and gently stir to combine.

6 Dump the bread mixture into the prepared baking dish. Sprinkle the remaining ½ cup cheese evenly over the top. Bake for 45 to 60 minutes, until the top is good and browned. You want the top of the bread and cheese to get crispy. To serve, let it cool slightly, then cut it into large squares and serve immediately. To serve leftovers, reheat the bread pudding in the oven instead of the microwave.

SMOKED SALMON FRITTATA

This frittata was inspired by two of my favorite things: bagels with lox and cream cheese, and my other favorite Jewish deli breakfast where onions are caramelized and then mixed with scrambled eggs and smoked salmon. I grew up eating at a super-classic deli in LA called Nate 'n Al, and they do this dish right. This is my homage to them. It does take some time to caramelize the onions, but it's *sooo* worth it to achieve that sweet, smoky taste.

10 large eggs

3 tablespoons whole milk

½ teaspoon fine sea salt

¼ cup cream cheese, at room temperature

1 teaspoon olive oil

½ cup chopped smoked salmon

1 onion, sliced and caramelized (see sidebar)

Chopped fresh chives, for garnish

1 Preheat the oven to 375°F.

2 In a medium bowl, whisk together the eggs and milk until bubbly. Add the salt and cream cheese and whisk to evenly break up the cream cheese into chunks.

3 In a large ovenproof skillet, heat the oil over medium heat. Add the salmon and caramelized onions. Stir to combine. Reduce the heat to low, then slowly pour the egg mixture into the skillet. Gently stir to combine and make sure everything is evenly distributed. Cook until the edges are set, about a minute or two.

4 Transfer the skillet to the oven and bake for 10 to 15 minutes, until the edges are golden and the center is set.

5 Let the frittata cool slightly in the pan, then slide it onto a plate and cut it into slices. Garnish the slices with chives and serve hot!

TO CARAMELIZE THE ONION

So, don't hate me . . . this process takes a while, but all good things come to those who wait, right?! Cut the onion into quarters, cut the quarters into long slices, then cut those slices in half. Place the onion in a small cast-iron or stainless steel skillet with no oil and set the pan over low to medium heat. Once the onions start releasing liquid and becoming translucent, reduce the heat to low, if it's not already there. The key to this process is *low and slow*. When they begin to brown too much or stick to the pan, add a tablespoon or two of water and stir, scraping up any bits stuck to the bottom of the pan. Don't worry—the water will cook off. Continue to do this as needed for the next hour. Once the onions are a deep, dark brown and soft, they are done.

SPINACH, ROASTED RED PEPPER, AND GOAT CHEESE FRITTATA

2 teaspoons olive oil

7 cups fresh spinach

1 teaspoon fine sea salt

10 large eggs

3 tablespoons goat cheese

Pinch of freshly ground black pepper

2 roasted red bell peppers (see sidebar)

Roasting the red peppers may seem like a lot of effort for a simple frittata recipe, but it adds such a nice deep flavor. Roasted red peppers and regular red peppers are two totally different animals, and in my opinion, roasted wins every time. Also note that carnivores can add bacon to this frittata for even more richness!

1 Preheat the oven to 375°F.

2 In a large ovenproof skillet, heat 1 teaspoon of the oil over medium heat. Add the spinach and ¾ teaspoon of the salt. Cook until the spinach is wilted and the moisture is drawn out. Transfer the spinach to a colander and let it cool slightly, then squeeze out all the liquid and set the spinach aside on a plate.

3 In a medium bowl, whisk the eggs until bubbly, then stir in the goat cheese, black pepper, and remaining ¼ teaspoon salt.

TO ROAST THE RED BELL PEPPERS

Preheat the oven to 500°F. Place 2 whole red bell peppers on a baking sheet and roast for 20 to 30 minutes, rotating the baking sheet halfway through the roasting time, until the skin is wrinkly, black, and charred. Remove the baking sheet from the oven, cover it immediately with foil, and let the peppers cool 10 to 15 minutes. Scrape off all the charred skin (if it's difficult to remove the skin, let the peppers cool a little longer) and remove and discard the stems and seeds. Chop the flesh of the peppers into small pieces.

4 In the skillet you used for the spinach, heat the remaining 1 teaspoon oil over medium heat. Add the spinach and roasted red peppers and stir to combine. Reduce the heat to low and slowly pour the egg mixture into the skillet. Gently stir to combine and make sure everything is evenly distributed. Cook until the edges are set, a minute or so. Transfer the skillet to the oven and bake for 10 to 15 minutes, until the edges are golden and the center is set.

5 Let the frittata cool slightly in the pan, then slide it onto a plate and cut it into slices. Serve hot!

PANCETTA AND ASPARAGUS FRITTATA

This is probably my favorite of all the frittatas—but *shhh*, don't tell the others. The saltiness of the pancetta combines with the earthy asparagus and almost sweet Asiago cheese—it's Italian-inspired perfection. Simple and straightforward, but flavorful.

8 large eggs

3 tablespoons whole milk

½ cup shredded aged Asiago cheese (can substitute Parmesan or even a sharp aged white Cheddar)

¼ teaspoon fine sea salt

Generous pinch of freshly ground black pepper

1 tablespoon olive oil

4 ounces pancetta (not thinly sliced), cubed

⅓ cup finely chopped shallots

10 stalks asparagus, tough ends removed, cut on an angle into ¼-inch-thick pieces

1 Preheat the oven to 375°F.

2 In a medium bowl, whisk together the eggs and milk until bubbly. Stir in the cheese, salt, and pepper and set aside.

3 In a large ovenproof skillet, heat the oil over medium heat. Add the pancetta and cook for a few minutes, until the pancetta just starts to turn slightly brown. Add the shallots and cook for another few minutes, until they start to become slightly translucent and aromatic. Add the asparagus and cook just until the asparagus starts to turn a deeper green; it should still be crisp. Reduce the heat to low and slowly pour the egg mixture into the skillet. Gently stir to combine and make sure everything is evenly distributed. Cook until the edges are set, about a minute or so.

4 Transfer the skillet to the oven and bake for 10 to 15 minutes, until the edges are golden and the center is set.

5 Let the frittata cool slightly in the pan, then slide it onto a plate and cut it into slices. Serve hot!

EGG IN A HOLE

This super-simple egg dish is fun for the whole family. Believe it or not, I had never eaten an "egg in a hole" until much later in life—like, in-my-thirties later. My life was forever changed, and I still have no clue how this classic easy way to serve eggs slipped past me for so long. I love to top them off with some Frank's RedHot sauce, but hey, have fun and do your own thing—add whatever sauce you like, or none at all.

1 slice whole wheat bread or your preferred bread

1 tablespoon unsalted butter

1 large egg

Pinch of fine sea salt

Pinch of freshly ground black pepper

Frank's RedHot or other hot sauce (optional)

OH, EGGS, HOW DO I LOVE THEE . . . LET ME COUNT THE WAYS

In 1898, Adolphe Meyer wrote the book *Eggs, and How to Use Them: A Guide for the Preparation of Eggs*, in which he presented *five hundred* ways to cook eggs. "Without the aid of eggs," he wrote, "the artistic cook would have to abandon his profession in despair." There's also an old chef's tale that the one hundred pleats in a chef's toque represent the one hundred ways to prepare an egg. The possibilities are almost endless. Time to think about raising some chickens!

1   Using a 2-inch cookie cutter, cut a hole in the center of the bread slice (or just tear out a hole in the center of the bread, but be sure to leave a border of bread intact all the way around).

2   In a skillet, melt ½ tablespoon of the butter over medium-high heat until just beginning to bubble. Reduce the heat to medium. Place the bread in the pan and slide it around to soak up the butter.

3   Crack the egg into the hole in the bread and sprinkle it with the salt and pepper. Cook, undisturbed, for 3 to 4 minutes, until the egg is set and almost cooked. Add the remaining butter to the side of the skillet. With a spatula, lift the bread and egg to let the butter melt, tilting the skillet to coat. Flip the bread back into the pan and cook for another minute, until the white is set but the yolk is still runny.

4   I like to top mine off with some Frank's RedHot sauce, but it's just as good on its own.

NOTE
If the egg cups sink in the center after you take them out of the oven, put them back in and bake them for a few minutes longer. I was surprised at how long they needed to cook, even when they looked done.

BAKED EGG CUPS

These take no time at all to prepare! They are so quick and easy to grab and go. Reheat them in the microwave for about 30 seconds and—done! Get creative with the ingredients. Anything goes! Have fun. You can even use the frittata recipes on pages 33, 34, and 36. Simply divide the frittata mixture evenly among the muffin cups. You can serve the egg cups in paper liners to make them even easier to take on the run . . . or just to make them cute.

Butter or nonstick cooking spray, for the pan (optional)

4 large eggs

2 tablespoons whole milk

½ teaspoon fine sea salt

3 tablespoons shredded cheese of your choice

1 Preheat the oven to 350°F. Lightly grease six wells of a muffin tin with butter or nonstick spray or line them with paper liners.

2 In a medium bowl, whisk together the eggs, milk, and salt until frothy. Fill each muffin cup three-quarters full with the egg mixture. Sprinkle about 1½ teaspoons of the cheese on top of each. Bake for 20 to 25 minutes, until golden brown on top.

HAM AND CHEESE EGG CUPS Sprinkle about 1 tablespoon chopped ham into each muffin cup before adding the egg mixture. Add the egg mixture, top each cup with 1½ teaspoons shredded Cheddar cheese, and bake as directed.

SPINACH AND TOMATO EGG CUPS Sprinkle 1 tablespoon chopped fresh spinach and 1 quartered cherry or grape tomato into each muffin cup before adding the egg mixture. Add the egg mixture, top each cup with 1½ teaspoons shredded Jack cheese, and bake as directed.

ZUCCHINI AND MUSHROOM EGG CUPS Chop 3 (¼-inch-thick) slices zucchini and 2 mushrooms and divide them evenly among each muffin cup before adding the egg mixture. Add the egg mixture, top each cup with 1½ teaspoons shredded Parmesan cheese, and bake as directed.

FENNEL SAUSAGE AND MUSHROOM QUICHE

I wanted to turn the classic savory flavor of ravioli into a breakfast dish. I knew the taste and texture of the sausage and shrooms would pair well with a hearty pie crust—thus, a quiche was born! Use this pie crust recipe for any sweet or savory dish that needs a crust.

PIE CRUST

2½ cups all-purpose flour

1½ tablespoons sugar

½ teaspoon fine sea salt

1¼ cups (2½ sticks) unsalted butter, cubed and chilled

2 large eggs

QUICHE

8 large eggs

½ cup whole milk

½ cup heavy cream

Pinch of freshly ground black pepper

¾ teaspoon fine sea salt

¾ cup shredded Comté cheese (can substitute Parmesan or even a sharp aged white Cheddar)

1½ tablespoons unsalted butter

9 ounces ground pork sausage

1 teaspoon fennel seeds, coarsely chopped

8 baby bella (cremini) mushrooms, sliced

2 large fresh sage leaves, finely chopped

1   **To make the pie crust:** In a food processor (or a large bowl, if mixing by hand), combine the flour, sugar, and salt. Pulse once or twice to combine. Add the butter and pulse until it is broken down into pea-size pieces. (If mixing by hand, get in there with your hands and work the butter into the flour.)

2   Add the eggs and pulse (or stir by hand) until combined. The dough may still seem dry and not entirely together—that's okay. Dump it out onto a piece of plastic wrap. Bring the dough together into a ball and flatten it into a disc on the plastic wrap; it should come together as you do, but if it is still too dry, add a teaspoon or two of very cold water. Wrap the dough tightly and refrigerate for at least 1 hour.

NOTE   This recipe will leave you with leftover dough. You can wrap and freeze it. This is also my recipe for pie dough, so you're welcome! Use this for your pie making!

3   Preheat the oven to 375°F.

4   On a well-floured work surface, roll out the dough into a round just under ¼ inch thick. Line a 9-inch pie pan with the dough (see Note). Cut the excess dough from the edge and then crimp the edge and fold it up. With a fork, gently poke the bottom of the dough all over. Line the dough with a large piece of parchment paper and fill it with dried beans or pie weights. Bake for 15 to 20 minutes, until it starts getting golden and is almost fully cooked. Remove the parchment and beans or weights and bake for 10 minutes more, or until just lightly golden all over and fully baked. Transfer to a wire rack; keep the oven on.

5   ***To make the quiche:*** In a medium bowl, whisk the eggs well until frothy. Add the milk, cream, pepper, and ¼ teaspoon of the salt and whisk again. Add the cheese and stir to combine. Set aside.

6   In a large skillet, melt 1 tablespoon of the butter over medium to high heat. Add the sausage, fennel seeds, and remaining ½ teaspoon salt and cook until the sausage is almost fully cooked, 8 to 10 minutes. Add the mushrooms and remaining ½ tablespoon butter and cook until the mushrooms begin to soften and the sausage is fully cooked all the way through, about 5 minutes. Add the sage and stir to combine.

7   Pour the sausage-mushroom mixture into the baked pie crust and spread it evenly. Pour the milk mixture evenly over the sausage and mushrooms.

8   Bake the quiche for 35 to 45 minutes, then cover it with foil and bake for 10 to 15 minutes more, until the center is jiggly but set.

9   Let the quiche cool, then slice and enjoy. The quiche will keep, covered, in the fridge for up to 3 days. Reheat it in the oven or microwave.

BRUSSELS SPROUT AND LEEK QUICHE

Let's be real here—you need to eat your greens. I have big dreams of going vegetarian, maybe even vegan. So . . . vegan might be a stretch for now, but at least this particular quiche has no extra protein added and features vegetables as the star. I have a hard time imagining not eating eggs (you're shocked, right?). The main reason I am raising my own chickens is so I know the eggs are coming from humanely raised—well, let's be honest—*spoiled* chickens with an organic diet.

8 large eggs

½ cup whole milk

½ cup heavy cream

1 teaspoon fine sea salt

¾ cup shredded Gruyère cheese

1½ tablespoons olive oil

1¾ cups chopped Brussels sprouts

About 1 large leek, halved, rinsed well, and sliced crosswise into ¼-inch-thick pieces (1 cup)

½ teaspoon red pepper flakes

1 tablespoon white wine vinegar

1 baked pie crust (see page 40)

1   Preheat the oven to 375°F.

2   In a medium bowl, whisk the eggs until frothy. Add the milk, cream, and ½ teaspoon of the salt and whisk again. Add the cheese and stir to combine. Set aside.

3   In a large skillet, heat the oil over medium to high heat. Add the Brussels sprouts and the remaining ½ teaspoon salt. Cook for about 8 minutes, until the Brussels sprouts just start to become tender. Add the leek and red pepper flakes. Cook for 5 to 8 minutes more. You want the Brussels sprouts to still have a bite to them, so don't overcook them. Add the vinegar and stir to combine.

4   Pour the Brussels sprouts and leeks into the baked pie crust and spread them evenly. Pour the milk mixture evenly over the Brussels sprouts and leek.

5   Bake the quiche for 35 to 45 minutes, then cover it with foil and bake for 10 to 15 minutes more, until the center is jiggly but set.

6   Let the quiche cool, then slice and enjoy. The quiche will keep, covered, in the fridge for up to 3 days. Reheat it in the oven or microwave.

EGG OBSESSIONS & OTHER SAVORIES

43

THE *BREAKFAST BURRITO*

If you don't love a breakfast burrito, I'm sorry, but we definitely cannot be friends—or maybe you just haven't had a good one. I'm always on the search for a great breakfast burrito, and I've discovered it's harder to find than you'd think. Lots try to claim the title, but most don't succeed. Sometimes you just have to take things into your own hands! So here is one I hope you find satisfying that you can make right at home. Feel free to add avocado and/or cheese if that's your thing.

1½ cups chopped creamer potatoes or quartered baby potatoes

4 slices bacon

2 tablespoons vegetable oil or canola oil

½ cup chopped onion (about ¼ onion)

½ cup chopped red bell pepper

½ cup chopped green bell pepper

¾ teaspoon smoked paprika

¼ teaspoon chili powder

1½ teaspoons fine sea salt

6 large eggs

2 tablespoons whole milk

1 tablespoon unsalted butter or vegetable oil or canola oil

3 (10-inch) flour tortillas

½ cup to ⅔ cup pico de gallo

Hot sauce (I like Cholula)

1   In a large pot, bring 4 cups water to a boil. Add the potatoes and cook for 5 to 10 minutes, until the potatoes are fork-tender.

2   Meanwhile, in a large skillet, cook the bacon until done and crispy, about 10 minutes or more. Transfer it to a plate lined with paper towels to drain excess fat and cool. Chop the cooled bacon into ½-inch pieces. Drain the potatoes and set aside.

3   In a large skillet, heat the oil over medium to high heat. Add the onion and bell peppers and cook for 5 minutes, until the onion is translucent and the bell peppers are soft. Add the potatoes, paprika, chili powder, and 1 teaspoon of the salt to the skillet. Cook for 5 to 10 minutes. Remove the skillet from the heat and cover it to keep warm.

4   In a medium bowl, whisk together the eggs, milk, and remaining ½ teaspoon salt until frothy. In a medium to large nonstick skillet, melt the butter over medium heat. Add the eggs and cook them as directed on page 26. Just before the eggs finish cooking, add them to the skillet with the potato mixture. Stir to combine and heat over low heat, until the eggs are cooked through but still wet-looking.

5   Spoon one-third of the scrambled egg mixture onto the bottom third of a tortilla in a rectangle. On top of the egg mixture, spoon about 3 tablespoons of pico de gallo and add three or four shakes of hot sauce. Fold the bottom third up toward the top, fold in the sides, and roll tightly. Repeat to fill the remaining tortillas.

6   Heat a medium nonstick skillet over medium heat. Place the burrito in the pan, seam-side down, and toast until it's crispy and golden brown, about 1 minute. Flip and repeat on the other side, then serve. Repeat to toast the remaining burritos.

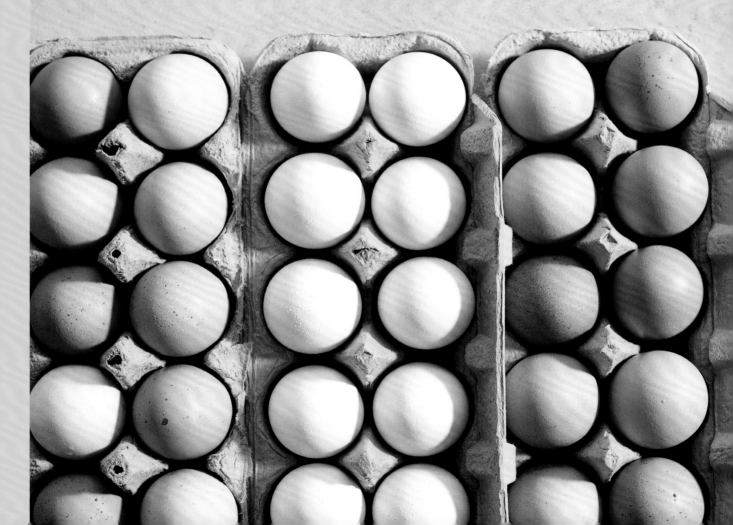

EGGS BENEDICT WITH HOLLANDAISE SAUCE (THREE WAYS)

HOLLANDAISE SAUCE

3 egg yolks

Juice of ½ lemon

½ teaspoon Dijon mustard

Pinch of cayenne pepper, plus more for garnish

½ teaspoon fine sea salt (see Notes, page 48)

7 tablespoons butter, sliced

EGGS BENEDICT

1 tablespoon distilled white vinegar

2 English muffins, split

4 large eggs (see Notes, page 48)

4 slices cooked ham, 4 slices smoked salmon, or 16 stalks steamed asparagus (see Notes, page 48)

Fresh dill or chopped chives, for garnish

This recipe includes an adaptation of my brother Merlin's blender hollandaise sauce, which originated from the *Joy of Cooking* hollandaise recipe. As a family tradition that started when Merlin and I were in our twenties, after opening presents on Christmas morning, my brother would make eggs Benedict for everyone using the leftover ham from our Christmas Eve dinner. To use his words, not mine, he didn't ever contribute much to the holiday, so this was his way of making up for it, and I'll tell ya, it earned my forgiveness—at least for a day. We would then proceed to lounge around and watch TV and sleep the rest of the day in our ugly Christmas pajamas (also a Christmas tradition in our family).

1   Fill a medium to large pot with 4 inches of water. Bring the water to a rolling boil. Reduce the heat to maintain a simmer and cover the pot.

2   **To make the hollandaise sauce:** In a blender, combine the egg yolks, lemon juice, mustard, cayenne, and salt and blend it briefly to combine. In a small skillet or pot, melt the sliced butter over medium heat. Once it's almost fully melted and starting to bubble but there are still a few pieces of solid butter remaining, remove it from the heat. (Please note: Do *not* melt the butter in the microwave, as you don't have control over the temperature and the temperature is key for making this blender hollandaise sauce.)

recipe continues

3 With the lid on the blender, turn it on low to medium speed, then slowly and carefully remove the cap in the lid (keeping the lid on) and pour in a little butter. Blend until the butter is incorporated, then with the blender running, carefully pour in the rest of the butter, little by little. Be careful, because this can splatter and make a very big mess! The mixture should instantly thicken up and create a delicious smooth hollandaise sauce. If it fails to thicken up right away, blend it on really high speed for a minute.

4 Keep the hollandaise sauce in the blender jar and give it a quick blend every minute or so or place the blender jar in a large bowl of warm water to keep the sauce warm so a film doesn't form on the top.

5 *To make the eggs Benedict:* Take the lid off the pot of water and add the vinegar.

6 Put the English muffin halves in the toaster. The English muffins and eggs will take the same amount of time, so you want to have the English muffins toasted and ready when the eggs finish cooking.

7 Crack one of the eggs into a small bowl. With a spoon, give the simmering water in the pot a quick clockwise stir so there is a little movement in the water. Once the water has almost stopped swirling, gently and carefully dip the bowl into the top of the water and dump the egg into the water. Without agitating the water again, repeat with the other eggs. Poach the eggs for 3 to 4 minutes. You want the whites to be completely set but the yolks to still be jiggly.

8 Place a slice of ham, a slice of smoked salmon, or 4 stalks of cooked asparagus on top of each toasted English muffin half.

9 Pull each egg out of the water with a slotted spoon. Give it a little shake to let the water drain off, then place it on top of the prepared English muffin. Top each with a couple of generous spoonfuls of the hollandaise sauce. Garnish with a quick shake of cayenne and dill or chives, and you are ready to enjoy!

NOTES If using smoked salmon in the Benedict, reduce the salt in the hollandaise sauce to ¼ teaspoon, as the smoked salmon is naturally salty.

I like to poach my eggs no more than four at a time so they don't overcrowd the pot. If you want to poach more than four eggs, you can reserve your first batch of poached eggs in a flat shallow bowl with a little bit of warm water in the bottom. Drain them when ready to serve.

To prepare the asparagus, if using: Place the stalks of asparagus in a shallow skillet with ½ inch of water and bring to a simmer over medium heat. Cook until the asparagus is a nice bright green and fork-tender, 3 to 5 minutes.

CHILAQUILES

2 dried pasilla peppers, stemmed and seeded

1 cup canned diced tomato with juice, or 3 fresh tomatoes, diced

½ cup chopped onion (about ¼ onion)

1 garlic clove

⅛ teaspoon ground cloves

¾ teaspoon fine sea salt, plus more as needed

1 tablespoon plus 2 teaspoons vegetable oil or canola oil, plus more for frying

10 corn tortillas, cut into triangle-shaped quarters, preferably stale

1 tablespoon sugar

1 teaspoon molasses

2 large eggs

Chopped fresh cilantro, for garnish

2 tablespoons chopped red onion, reserved in water then drained before serving, for garnish

2 to 3 tablespoons crumbled cotija cheese, for garnish

Mexican crema, for garnish

Oh, *chilaquiles,* I love you. The first time I was introduced to these half-crispy, half-soggy tortilla chips soaked in salsa and topped with a runny egg, I just about lost my mind, and my hangover was instantly cured. My favorite kind of *chilaquiles* are made with mole sauce, but that is an involved art with lots of ingredients, so I'll leave it to the experts. This is the next best thing. I use the same peppers they use in mole to give it richness and then add a little sugar and molasses to give it a unique edge of flavor that, if I might say so myself, makes these *chilaquiles* the best I've had without traditional mole.

1   In a small dry skillet, toast the pasilla peppers over medium to high heat for 2 to 3 minutes, just until they become aromatic. Transfer them to a small pot and add just enough water to cover them. Bring the water to a boil, turn off the heat, and let the peppers sit for 10 minutes.

2   In a blender, combine the tomato, onion, garlic, cloves, the pasilla peppers and ¾ cup of the cooking liquid from the pot, and the salt and blend until smooth. Pour the chile sauce into a bowl and set aside.

3   Fill a medium pot with oil to a depth of 1 inch and clip a thermometer to the side. Heat the oil over medium to high heat until it reaches 350°F. (If you don't have a thermometer, test the temperature with a piece of tortilla: Dip a corner of the tortilla piece into the oil. If it bubbles, the oil is hot enough.) Gently place a handful of tortilla pieces into the hot oil, being careful not to overcrowd the pot, and separate them with a heatproof slotted spoon or strainer (you don't want the pieces to stick together). Fry the tortilla pieces until they are golden brown, tossing and flipping them over in the oil once or twice

recipe continues

EGG OBSESSIONS & OTHER SAVORIES

49

while they cook. Using the slotted spoon, remove the tortilla chips from the pot, allowing the oil to drain off, and place them on a plate lined with paper towels. Immediately sprinkle the chips with salt. Repeat with the remaining tortilla pieces, working in batches.

4 Add the sugar and molasses to the chile sauce and stir to combine.

5 In a large skillet, heat 1 tablespoon of the oil over medium to high heat. Add the chile sauce. Bring to a simmer and cook for 5 minutes, or until the sauce starts to thicken a little bit. Reduce the heat to low to keep the sauce warm.

6 In a small nonstick skillet, heat the remaining 2 teaspoons oil. Add the eggs and fry until the whites are mostly set with a little bit of the white around the yolk still runny. Turn off the heat just before the eggs are done, as they will continue to cook in the skillet. Leave the eggs in the skillet. If you need to place a lid on the pan to help the eggs cook the rest of the way, you can. This will ensure the whites are fully set but the yolks are still runny by the time you're ready to assemble the plate.

7 Add the tortilla chips to the skillet of chile sauce and stir to combine, making sure all the chips are covered and soaked with the sauce. Turn off the heat.

8 Spoon out the chips and place them on a large serving plate, or divide them between two individual plates. Add the fried eggs to the top of the pile of chips. (If you divided them between two plates, place one fried egg on each.)

9 Top with cilantro, the red onion, and the cotija cheese, and drizzle with crema. Enjoy.

EGGS IN PURGATORY

Any time you serve any sort of tomato-based sauce that's meant to be sopped up with bread, I'm all in! There are few things better, in my opinion. So here is breakfast's version, with a little bit of spice to heat things up.

3 tablespoons olive oil, plus more as needed

½ cup grape or cherry tomatoes

1 cup chopped onion (about ½ large onion)

½ cup chopped roasted red bell pepper (see page 34)

4 large garlic cloves, minced

1 (28-ounce) can diced tomatoes, with their juices

2 tablespoons capers, plus 2 tablespoons caper brine from the jar

½ teaspoon red pepper flakes (or less if you prefer less heat)

1 teaspoon fine sea salt

4 large eggs

4 (¾-inch-thick) slices country or French bread

¼ cup shredded Parmesan cheese

2 to 3 tablespoons chopped fresh basil, for garnish

1 In a 10-inch cast-iron skillet or other skillet, heat the oil over medium-high heat. Add the grape tomatoes and cook for 5 minutes, until they start to burst and soften. Be careful, as the oil can splatter when the tomatoes burst.

2 Add the onion and cook for a few minutes, until translucent. Add the roasted red pepper and the garlic. Cook, stirring, for a couple of minutes, until the garlic becomes very fragrant but not browned.

3 Add the diced tomatoes with their juices and bring the mixture to a boil. Add the capers, caper brine, red pepper flakes, and salt. Reduce the heat to maintain a high simmer. You want the sauce still bubbling to poach the eggs.

4 Crack one of the eggs into a small bowl. Make a hole in the sauce with a large spoon, then pour the egg into the hole. Repeat with the remaining eggs. Place a lid loosely over the skillet and cook for 4 to 6 minutes, until the egg whites are set but the yolks are still runny. While the eggs are cooking, generously drizzle the bread with oil and toast it until crispy and browned.

5 Once the eggs are done, remove the skillet from the heat. Sprinkle the cheese and basil over the top and drizzle with oil. Serve family-style with everyone digging into the skillet, or serve on plates—whatever makes you happy. Scoop up with the bread and enjoy!

SWEET POTATO HASH WITH EGGS

1½ teaspoons fine sea salt, plus more as needed

4 cups small-diced sweet potatoes (about 2 medium-large potatoes)

5 tablespoons vegetable oil or canola oil

¼ teaspoon freshly ground black pepper, plus more as needed

1 small red onion, finely chopped (about 1½ cups)

1 red bell pepper, finely chopped (about 1 cup)

1 small green bell pepper, finely chopped (about 1 cup)

½ teaspoon chili powder

1 pound ground turkey

¾ teaspoon smoked paprika

Pinch of cayenne pepper (more or less, depending on your preferred level of spice)

2 garlic cloves, finely chopped

6 drops of Tabasco sauce

2 large eggs

Finely chopped scallions, for garnish

To me, nothing says "breakfast" more than a sultry combination of meat, potatoes, and eggs. And nothing beats a great hash for accomplishing this trifecta. This is my attempt at offering a lighter, healthier version of this classic breakfast combo. Feel free to dirty it up by adding a package of bacon, cooked and chopped, or subbing out the turkey for ground beef.

1   Bring a large pot of salted water to a boil. Add the sweet potatoes and cook for about 2 minutes, until just tender. Drain the potatoes, run them under cold water, and place them on a plate to dry (pat them dry with paper towels or a clean kitchen towel, if needed).

2   In a large skillet, heat 2 tablespoons of the oil over high heat. Add the sweet potatoes, a pinch of black pepper, and ½ teaspoon of the salt. Cook for about 10 minutes, until the potatoes begin to brown and even blacken some. Place them on a plate and set aside.

3   In the same skillet, heat 2 tablespoons of the oil over medium to high heat. Add the onion and bell peppers and cook until browned. Don't be afraid to let them blacken a little, too, but be careful not to let them burn. Remove them from the pan and set aside.

4   In the same skillet, heat the remaining 1 tablespoon oil. In a small bowl, combine the remaining 1 teaspoon salt, the black pepper, and ¼ teaspoon of the chili powder. Season both sides of the slab of ground turkey with the salt mixture. Add the turkey to the skillet and cook, breaking it up with a spoon, until cooked all the way through, about 6 to 8 minutes.

5 Return the sweet potatoes, onion, and bell peppers to the skillet with the turkey. Reduce the heat to medium-low. Stir in the smoked paprika, cayenne, garlic, and remaining ¼ teaspoon chili powder. Cook for about 5 minutes to allow the flavors to develop. Add the Tabasco and stir to combine. Taste and season with additional salt and black pepper if needed. Reduce the heat to low to keep warm.

6 In a separate pan, fry the eggs sunny-side up (see page 29).

7 Serve the hash topped with the eggs and garnished with the scallions.

HUEVOS RANCHEROS

1 teaspoon chopped canned chipotle chile in adobo sauce, plus 1 teaspoon adobo sauce from the can

1 (14.5-ounce) can fire-roasted diced tomatoes

1 tablespoon canned diced green chile

¼ cup plus 2 tablespoons vegetable oil or canola oil

½ cup chopped onion (about ½ onion)

1 garlic clove, minced

Pinch of freshly ground black pepper

¼ teaspoon dried oregano

1 to 3 dashes of Tabasco sauce, or more if you like it spicy

½ teaspoon fine sea salt

4 white corn tortillas

4 large eggs

1 (15-ounce) can black beans, drained, rinsed, and warmed

Crumbled cotija cheese, for garnish

Chopped fresh cilantro, for garnish

½ avocado, chopped, for garnish

If I wrote a breakfast cookbook and did not include huevos rancheros, I think my mom would disown me. She likes the super-traditional version, but I prefer this modern California style. After all, I'm a Southern California girl. There is a little bit of smoke from the chipotle chile that does give the dish a nice traditional nod. That's for you, Mom!

1   In a blender, combine the chipotle chile, adobo sauce, diced tomatoes, and green chile. Blend until somewhat smooth but still a little chunky.

2   In a skillet, heat 1 tablespoon of the oil over medium to high heat. Add the onion and cook for 3 to 5 minutes, until the onion begins to soften. Add the tomato mixture. Bring to a boil, then reduce the heat to maintain a simmer.

3   Add the garlic, pepper, oregano, Tabasco, and salt. Reduce the heat to low and cover the skillet.

4   In a shallow pot or skillet, heat ¼ cup of the oil. Add 2 tortillas at a time and fry for about 1 minute per side, until the tortillas are somewhat crispy and lightly golden but still soft. We're going for a crispy and chewy texture.

5   Place 2 tortillas on each plate.

6   In a separate large skillet, heat the remaining 1 tablespoon oil and fry the eggs sunny-side up (see page 29).

7   Top the tortillas on each plate with a good amount of black beans, a generous amount of the tomato sauce, then 2 fried eggs, then a little more sauce on top of the eggs. Finish with the cotija cheese, cilantro, and avocado.

GALLO PINTO (COSTA RICAN RICE AND BEANS)

This is an homage to my three years living in Costa Rica, where I opened my very first restaurant. I was twenty-five. I could barely communicate with my employees—my Spanish was awful. It was a lot of smiling and nodding. I wish I had learned how to make this authentic Tico dish, Gallo Pinto (which translates to "painted rooster"), from Doña Maruja, my prep cook, line cook, dishwasher, and all-around savior. She made it best, and it was one of the most popular dishes on our breakfast menu. But I didn't ask her, as I was barely holding my head above water while learning to speak a new language, figuring out how to bake in 100° heat with 100% humidity . . . the list goes on! When I didn't get it at my restaurant, I would pay about $3 for it at the local *soda* (casual restaurant), and then I'd eat it while sitting amid the jungle, with waves crashing in the background and the sounds of howler monkeys in the trees.

11 tablespoons vegetable oil or canola oil

1¼ cups chopped onion

1 cup chicken stock

1 cup rice

1 cup finely chopped red bell pepper

1 (15-ounce) can reduced-sodium black beans, undrained

¼ teaspoon celery salt

¼ teaspoon onion powder

¼ teaspoon mustard powder

1 teaspoon sugar

1 teaspoon fine sea salt

2 tablespoons finely chopped fresh cilantro

1 ripe plantain (the blacker the plantain skin, the better and sweeter) or banana, sliced on an angle ½ inch thick

8 large eggs

Crumbled cotija cheese or Mexican crema, for garnish

Salsa Lizano (see Note, page 59), for serving

1 In a medium pot, heat 2 tablespoons of the oil over medium to high heat. Add ¾ cup of the onion and cook for a few minutes, until the onion is translucent and aromatic. Add 1½ cups water and the stock and bring to a boil. Add the rice. Bring the liquid back to a boil, then reduce the heat to maintain a simmer, cover, and cook for 20 to 30 minutes, until the rice has absorbed all the liquid and is soft but not mushy. Check the rice for doneness after 20 minutes and give it a stir to make sure it's not sticking to the bottom of the pan. If it is the tiniest bit still undercooked, turn off the heat and leave the pot covered; the rice will continue to cook in the residual heat and will cook further when you add it to the beans and peppers.

2 In a large skillet, heat 3 tablespoons of the oil over medium to high heat. Add the bell pepper and the remaining ½ cup onion and cook for 5 to 8 minutes, until the onion is translucent and the pepper begins to soften. Add the beans with the liquid from the can, the celery salt, onion powder, mustard powder, sugar, and sea salt and stir to combine.

3 Add 2 cups of the cooked rice to the skillet and stir to combine (save the remaining rice for another use). Cook for a couple of minutes more, until everything is heated through. Turn off the heat, stir in the cilantro, and cover the skillet to keep warm.

4 To fry the plantain (this is my favorite part of this dish!), in a medium skillet, heat 4 tablespoons of the oil over medium to high heat. Add the plantain pieces and fry for 3 to 4 minutes on each side, until nicely golden brown. Set them aside on a plate lined with paper towels.

5 In a large skillet, heat the remaining 2 tablespoons oil over medium heat. Add 4 of the eggs, fry them to your liking, then repeat with the remaining 4 eggs.

6 Divide the rice among four plates. Serve each topped with 2 fried eggs, sprinkled with cotija cheese or crema, drizzled with Salsa Lizano, and with a few slices of fried plantain alongside. Enjoy.

NOTE The real key to this dish is the sauce you serve it with: Salsa Lizano. It might be one of Costa Rica's most famous things. It is delicious and otherworldly. If you've had it, you know. If you haven't, then say thanks to Amazon, because now you can order it.

QUINOA AND BLACK BEAN MEXICAN BREAKFAST BOWL

This super-hearty and healthy breakfast bowl is my go-to. It's easy to make the quinoa mix ahead of time and eat it whenever and with whatever you choose. I try to avoid rice whenever possible, so quinoa is a perfect substitute as well as one of the few perfect vegetarian proteins. On its own, it's not quite hearty enough for me, so I add some black beans and veggies and voilà!

SAUCE

¼ cup reduced-fat sour cream

1 tablespoon hot sauce (I prefer Cholula; use less if you prefer less heat)

Pinch of fine sea salt

BREAKFAST BOWL

1 cup uncooked quinoa

2 tablespoons olive oil

1 cup small-diced red onion (½ large or 1 small onion), with 1 to 2 tablespoons finely chopped onion reserved in water for garnish

½ cup small-diced red bell pepper

1 garlic clove, minced

6 to 8 large eggs, cooked sunny-side up (see page 29; 2 per serving)

1 (15-ounce) can black beans, drained and rinsed

½ teaspoon fine sea salt

1 lime, quartered

1 bunch cilantro, chopped

Pico de gallo

1 avocado, sliced

1 *To make the sauce:* In a small bowl, combine the sour cream, hot sauce, and salt and set aside.

2 *To make the breakfast bowl:* Cook the quinoa according to the instructions on the package.

3 Meanwhile, in a large skillet, heat the oil over medium-high heat. Set 1 to 2 tablespoons of the diced onion aside in a small bowl with water to cover. Add the remaining onion, the bell pepper, and the garlic to the skillet. Cook for 2 to 3 minutes, then remove from the heat.

4 Meanwhile, cook the eggs sunny-side up according to the instructions on page 29.

5 Drain the reserved onion.

6 Add the cooked quinoa, black beans, and salt to the skillet with the onion-pepper mixture. Stir to combine.

7 Spoon the quinoa mixture onto three or four plates or shallow bowls. Squeeze a lime wedge over each. Top each with 2 sunny-side-up eggs, and divide the cilantro, pico de gallo, reserved onion, avocado, and sauce among them. Enjoy!

MAPLE BREAKFAST SAUSAGE

I am not really a breakfast sausage kinda person, but these babies have changed that. I eat more ground turkey than pork in my day-to-day life, so I wanted to do an equal mix of pork sausage and ground turkey to lighten these sausages up a bit. They are savory and flavorful, with just the right amount of maple-y sweetness.

1 pound ground pork

1 pound ground turkey

2 teaspoons fresh thyme leaves

1 teaspoon finely chopped fresh sage leaves

¼ teaspoon red pepper flakes

2 garlic cloves, minced

1 tablespoon finely grated white onion

½ teaspoon fine sea salt

¼ teaspoon freshly ground black pepper

¼ teaspoon mustard powder

¼ cup dark maple syrup

½ teaspoon maple extract

1 tablespoon vegetable oil or canola oil

1   Line a baking sheet with wax paper.

2   In a large bowl, combine all the ingredients except the vegetable oil. With your hands, work everything together to evenly combine and distribute the ingredients, being careful not to overwork the meat. I'm not gonna lie—it's messy, but you gotta get in there with your hands. It's the only way. Set those rings somewhere safe, ladies.

3   Take ¼- to ⅓-cup portions of the mixture and shape them into patties. You can determine the size—I usually shape some into smaller rounds for eating the sausage on its own and some into larger, flatter patties for breakfast sandwiches. Place the patties on the baking sheet as you finish them. Cover them with another sheet of wax paper and refrigerate for 1 hour, then cook the sausages or freeze them for later use.

4   **To cook the sausages:** In a large skillet, heat the oil over medium to high heat. Once the oil is hot, add 4 or more patties. Reduce the heat to medium-low and cook for 4 to 6 minutes on each side, until cooked all the way through.

5   **To freeze the sausages:** Freeze the patties on the baking sheet for 4 to 6 hours, until they are almost frozen solid, then stack the patties, separated by squares of wax paper, and store them in an airtight container or freezer bag in the freezer for 1 month.

CHIPOTLE-MAPLE BREAKFAST SAUSAGE SANDWICH

So, I can't take credit for this sandwich—it was inspired by a restaurant in LA called Locali. At first I thought, *chipotle and maple? You're crazy.* But then I tried it—and it works. It works so well, I set out to create my own. Their version is vegan—this is definitely not. It's a spicy, sweet, smoky kinda thing that is just yummy!

CHIPOTLE SAUCE

¾ cup plain Greek yogurt

½ chipotle chile from a can, plus 2 teaspoons adobo sauce from the can

Pinch of fine sea salt

Squeeze of fresh lemon juice

SANDWICHES

1 tablespoon vegetable oil or canola oil

2 Maple Breakfast Sausage patties (page 62)

2 slices aged provolone cheese

2 large eggs

2 whole wheat English muffins

3 to 4 teaspoons maple syrup

1   ***To make the chipotle sauce:*** In a food processor, combine all the sauce ingredients and pulse until smooth and combined.

2   ***To make the sandwiches:*** In a medium skillet, heat the oil over medium to high heat. Add the sausage patties. Reduce the heat to medium-low and cook the sausages on the first side for 4 to 6 minutes, then flip and top each with a slice of cheese and cook for 4 to 6 minutes more, until cooked all the way through.

3   Meanwhile, in a separate medium skillet, fry the eggs. Toast the English muffins.

4   Spread chipotle sauce over a toasted English muffin half and top with an egg and one sausage patty. Drizzle 1½ teaspoons or so of maple syrup on the other English muffin half and close the sandwich. Repeat to make a second sandwich. Enjoy!

MY GO-TO BREAKFAST SANDWICH

This is the super-simple, healthier-than-normal egg sandwich I live on. The keys to this sandwich are to cook the eggs perfectly so the yolks are really runny and to use the Laughing Cow cheese. The Laughing Cow is creamy and cheesy, and low in calories. As I mentioned before, this is my healthy hack for *all* sandwiches. When the runny yolk combines with the creamy cheese, it is so indulgent. With the buttery crispiness of the sourdough plus the spice of the arugula, you've got yourself a pretty delicious, simple, and satisfying breakfast sandwich. Feel free to jazz it up to your liking by adding bacon or whatever you want.

2½ tablespoons unsalted butter

2 slices sourdough or whole wheat bread

2 large eggs

1 tablespoon Dijon mustard

1 wedge the Laughing Cow Light Creamy Swiss Cheese

Small handful of fresh arugula

1 or 2 slices fresh tomato

1   In a medium skillet, melt 1½ tablespoons of the butter over medium to high heat. Add both slices of bread and toast until golden brown on one side.

2   At the same time, in a small skillet, melt the remaining 1 tablespoon butter over medium to high heat. Add the eggs. Reduce the heat to medium and cook just until the whites are almost set. Turn off the heat and cover the skillet. The residual heat will finish cooking the eggs.

3   Spread the mustard over one slice of bread and spread the cheese on the other. Add the eggs, top with the arugula and tomato, sandwich together, and enjoy!

PREP TIME: 5 minutes   *TOTAL TIME:* 15 minutes   *YIELD:* Serves 2

PESTO-PROSCIUTTO BREAKFAST SANDWICH

This is my Italian American–inspired breakfast sandwich. It's indulgent. I love the bright flavor of the basil pesto with the salty prosciutto, oozy egg yolk, and super-cheesy melty goodness. This is a treat!

PESTO

½ cup olive oil

2½ cups fresh basil leaves

2 tablespoons pine nuts, lightly toasted

2 garlic cloves

½ cup grated Parmesan cheese

1 teaspoon chopped fresh parsley

½ teaspoon fine sea salt

SANDWICHES

4 slices sourdough bread

4 slices aged provolone cheese

4 slices prosciutto

4 tablespoons (½ stick) butter, at room temperature

4 large eggs

NOTE   You'll have a little leftover pesto, but you may want to double the pesto recipe so you have a lot extra, because it is super delicious and versatile. Use it on other sandwiches, bruschetta, pizza, and pasta.

1   **To make the pesto:** In a food processor, combine all the pesto ingredients. Pulse until somewhat smooth. Stop and scrape down the sides and bottom of the food processor as needed to make sure everything mixes together evenly.

2   **To make the sandwiches:** Spread a generous amount of pesto (1 to 2 tablespoons per slice) on 4 slices of bread. On 2 of the slices of bread, top the pesto with a slice of cheese, then 2 slices of prosciutto, then another slice of cheese. Close each sandwich.

3   In a large skillet, melt 2 tablespoons of the butter over medium heat. Place the sandwiches in the skillet and cook until golden brown on one side, 3 to 5 minutes. While the first side is browning, spread ½ tablespoon of butter over the top of each sandwich. Once the first side is browned, flip them over and cook until browned on the second side. (You are basically making a grilled cheese.)

4   Meanwhile, in a large skillet, melt the remaining 1 tablespoon butter. Add the eggs and cook sunny-side up according to the instructions on page 29.

5   Once the sandwiches and eggs are finished cooking, peel open each sandwich and place 2 eggs inside. Place each sandwich on a plate, cut them in half, and enjoy!

ROSEMARY-GARLIC BREAKFAST POTATOES

No brunch spread is complete without breakfast potatoes. They go with anything—simple scrambled eggs, eggs Benedict, as a savory pairing with pancakes, you name it. These take about an hour in the oven but are easy to have baking while all the other goodies are getting prepared. Make a big batch and eat 'em for breakfast *and* dinner.

3½ cups diced red potatoes (or a mix of red and small white potatoes)

1 tablespoon finely chopped fresh rosemary

½ teaspoon fine sea salt, plus more if needed

2 garlic cloves

Large pinch of freshly ground black pepper

3 tablespoons olive oil

1   Preheat the oven to 350°F. Line a baking sheet with foil.

2   Put all the ingredients on the prepared baking sheet and toss to combine. Bake for about 1 hour, tossing the potatoes every 15 minutes; be careful, as they may stick to the foil. Once the potatoes are a nice golden brown and crispy on the edges, they are ready.

3   Taste and add more salt, if desired, then serve.

SYRUP REQUIRED

BUTTERMILK PANCAKES

Pancakes are one of my comfort-food favorites—always *buttermilk* pancakes, in my opinion, and always worth the splurge of a super-high-quality real maple syrup. So simple, but so good. You have two options—you can either pour the pancake batter directly onto the griddle or pan without any butter, or you can melt 1 tablespoon butter in the pan first and *then* cook the pancakes. The difference is this: Cooking *without* butter gives you a soft outside that is evenly golden brown—think restaurant pancakes. Cooking *with* butter will give you a slightly crusty outside that is not necessarily perfectly even and golden brown. It's your preference. I leave it in your hands. I felt it my duty to share how restaurants were able to achieve such a uniformly perfect golden brown color on pancakes. A chef I worked with taught me the trick, and my mind was blown. You're welcome.

1 cup all-purpose flour

1½ tablespoons sugar

¾ teaspoon baking powder

¾ teaspoon baking soda

¾ teaspoon fine sea salt

1 large egg, separated

1¼ cups buttermilk

1 teaspoon vanilla extract

2 tablespoons unsalted butter, melted, plus more if needed

1 In a large bowl, whisk together the flour, sugar, baking powder, baking soda, and salt until thoroughly combined. Make a well in the center of the dry ingredients and set aside.

2 In a medium bowl, whisk the egg yolk into the buttermilk, then whisk in the vanilla, and finally the melted butter.

3 In a small bowl, whisk the egg white until frothy and lightly whipped (it should look like beer foam). Set aside.

4 Pour the buttermilk mixture into the center of the dry ingredients and gently fold to combine, without fully mixing. Add the egg white and gently mix until there are no streaks of dry flour left, but the batter is still lumpy.

5 Heat a large nonstick skillet or griddle over medium to high heat.

recipe continues

6 Pour ¼ to ½ cup of the batter onto the pan for each pancake and cook for about 3 minutes, until the top side of the pancakes are super bubbly, then flip them. (Another important tip: Flip with the wrist. Slide the spatula under the pancake and flip with your wrist, not your arm.) Cook for about 3 minutes on the second side, transfer to a plate, and repeat with the remaining batter.

WHOLE WHEAT BLUEBERRY BUTTERMILK PANCAKES Follow the recipe for Buttermilk Pancakes, replacing the all-purpose flour with ¾ cup whole wheat flour. Pour ¼ to ½ cup of the batter onto the skillet or griddle for each pancake. Sprinkle blueberries around the outside of each pancake, about 1 inch apart, then place 2 or 3 blueberries in the center. (Yes, this is me being a bit OCD, but you should have a blueberry in every bite. At my bakery, I actually made my bakers count the blueberries they put into each blueberry doughnut, and, yes, I checked. It is these little details that make all the difference.)

PREP TIME: 1 minute   **TOTAL TIME:** 20 minutes   **YIELD:** Makes 1½ cups, to serve 6 to 8

MIXED BERRY COMPOTE

Pair this compote with pancakes, waffles, and syrupy things in general.

½ cup chopped fresh strawberries	¼ cup sugar
½ cup fresh raspberries	1 teaspoon vanilla extract
½ cup fresh blueberries	½ teaspoon lemon zest
½ cup fresh blackberries	1 tablespoon fresh lemon juice

1 In a small saucepan, combine all the ingredients and cook over medium to high heat, mashing the mixture with a fork or potato masher to break up the fruit, for about 20 minutes, until the fruit breaks down and just starts to thicken. Be careful not to cook too long—we aren't going for a jam-like consistency. We are going for a less thick, chunky, fruity sauce.

2 Serve the compote warm on top of pancakes or waffles, or let it cool and store in an airtight container in the fridge for up to 1 week. It's also good on toast, yogurt, and ice cream.

WAFFLES

Waffles are surprisingly tricky. You want to get that balance of a crispy outside and a light-and-fluffy inside. My obsession with buttermilk comes from the fact that it provides a softer texture in any baked good, and the whipped egg white helps to achieve the fluffy factor essential to a good waffle. I opt for waffles when I want something syrupy and comforting but maybe not as heavy as a pancake. Waffles are also fun to use as bread for breakfast sandwiches.

1 cup all-purpose flour

½ teaspoon baking powder

½ teaspoon baking soda

2 tablespoons sugar

½ teaspoon fine sea salt

1 cup buttermilk

1 large egg

2 tablespoons unsalted butter, melted

1 egg white

Nonstick cooking spray

NOTE To keep waffles warm, preheat the oven to 200°F and line a baking sheet with a wire rack. Warm the waffles in the oven on the prepared baking sheet. This method is best to allow air circulation and keep the bottoms of the waffles from getting soggy. Just be sure not to stack the waffles on top of one another, or they'll get soggy anyway.

1 In a medium bowl, whisk together the flour, baking powder, baking soda, sugar, and salt until thoroughly combined, then make a well in the center of the dry ingredients and set aside.

2 Pour the buttermilk into a small bowl and set aside.

3 In a separate small bowl, beat the egg, then whisk in the melted butter. Add the egg mixture to the buttermilk and whisk until combined.

4 In the bowl you just used for the egg-butter mixture, whisk the egg white until it's frothy and lightly whipped (it should look like beer foam) and set aside.

5 Pour the buttermilk mixture into the well in the dry ingredients and stir until slightly combined. Add the egg white and gently mix until there are no streaks of dry flour left, but the batter is still lumpy.

6 Turn on a waffle maker and coat the plates with nonstick spray. Cook the batter according to the manufacturer's instructions, keeping in mind that you may need to cook the waffles longer than the instructions indicate. The waffles should be crispy and golden brown and should not still feel wet inside when poked. They should have some spring to them. Transfer the waffles to a plate and repeat with the remaining batter, making sure to spray the waffle iron with nonstick spray between batches.

NORMA'S RESTAURANT WA-ZA

This is one of the best, most creative breakfast dishes I have ever eaten or seen at a restaurant. It is right on the border between dessert and breakfast . . . and that is why, as a pastry chef, I love breakfast so much—because you can flirt with that line. This is my best version of it, and it is damn good, but I will still say, if you find yourself close to a Parker Hotel, in Palm Springs or New York City, go inside, sidle up to a table at Norma's Restaurant, and do yourself a favor: order the Wa-Za. Even the name is fun. Note: This dish is so crazy you need a blowtorch to make it! Really. No need to worry, though. A little kitchen torch will do the job just fine!

1 Waffle (page 73)

1 (6-ounce) container Yoplait strawberry or other flavored yogurt (yes, you need to use the sugary yogurt—it's just better for this)

1 banana, thinly sliced on an angle into long pieces

2 tablespoons sugar

Fresh raspberries and blueberries or other preferred fruit, for garnish

1 Place the waffle on a plate and pile the yogurt into the center in a layer about 1 inch high, leaving about a 1½-inch border uncovered.

2 Arrange the banana slices around the edges of the waffle, placing them on top of the outer edge of the yogurt so that the banana slices hang over the edges of the waffle.

3 Sprinkle the sugar over the yogurt and over about half the banana slices. Caramelize the sugar with the blowtorch until it's golden brown. Sprinkle with fresh raspberries and blueberries, and enjoy!

SYRUP REQUIRED

CHICKEN AND WAFFLES

One of the best sweet-and-savory combinations of all time. This is one of my favorite brunch items to order whenever it's on a menu. Once again . . . me and the buttermilk! But I promise it renders the chicken super moist and delicious (the longer you soak it, the better), and the twice-dipping gives an extra crunch. Cook up a big batch of fried chicken and eat it on waffles or have yourself some extra-crunchy chicken fingers. I have been known to quite frequently order chicken fingers off the kids' menu for myself . . . they are just too good!

2 cups buttermilk

1 pound raw chicken breast tenders

1 recipe Waffles (page 73; see Note, page 73)

Vegetable oil or canola oil, for frying

2 large eggs, beaten

1 cup all-purpose flour

¾ cup panko bread crumbs

¾ teaspoon paprika

½ teaspoon freshly ground black pepper

Large pinch or two of garlic salt

¾ teaspoon fine sea salt

1 to 2 cups grated sharp Cheddar cheese (optional)

Maple syrup, for serving

Frank's RedHot sauce, for serving

Sliced scallions, for garnish

1   Pour the buttermilk into a shallow dish and add the chicken tenders, turning them to coat as needed. Cover and refrigerate for at least 1 hour or up to overnight.

2   Preheat the oven to 200°F. Line a baking sheet with a wire rack.

3   Make the waffles and keep them warm in the oven on the prepared baking sheet (see Note, page 73) while you cook the chicken.

4   Fill a high-sided skillet with oil to a depth of 1 to 2 inches and clip a thermometer to the side. Heat the oil over medium to high heat until it reaches 350 to 360°F.

5   While the oil is heating, place the beaten eggs in a small, shallow dish. In a small baking pan or dish, combine the flour, panko, paprika, pepper, garlic salt, and sea salt. Stir well to combine.

6   Using tongs, remove one piece of chicken from the buttermilk and coat it on both sides in the flour mixture, then dip both sides in the egg, allowing any excess to drip off, then coat in the flour mixture again. Set aside on a large dish and repeat to coat the remaining chicken pieces.

recipe continues

7 Working in small batches, add a few pieces of chicken to the hot oil and fry for about 5 minutes on each side, until nicely golden brown. The frying time may vary depending on the size of the chicken pieces. Using tongs, transfer the chicken to a plate lined with paper towels. If desired, sprinkle a generous amount of the cheese over the fried chicken immediately after frying so it will melt from the residual heat. Repeat to fry the remaining chicken, adding cheese (if using) to each batch.

8 To serve, place the waffles on individual plates and top each with a piece or two of fried chicken. Cover in maple syrup and sprinkle with Frank's RedHot and scallions. Enjoy! Save any leftover chicken to eat as chicken fingers.

CLASSIC FRENCH TOAST

The classic French toast recipe . . . what's not to love? It's good on its own or as the perfect vessel for all sorts of additions. I like to use a thicker, richer bread like brioche or challah for my French toast, as it provides a lighter, fluffier texture. The key is to always make sure that whatever bread you choose is stale. If you are in a pinch, you can very, very, very lightly toast it, but it's best to leave the bread out overnight or for a few hours to make it stale.

4 large eggs

2 tablespoons whole milk

⅛ teaspoon ground cinnamon

4 (½-inch-thick) slices stale bread (I prefer brioche or challah)

1 tablespoon unsalted butter

1 In a large shallow bowl, whisk together the eggs, milk, and cinnamon.

2 Soak the slices of bread in the egg mixture for 30 to 45 seconds on each side, then set aside on a plate.

3 In a large skillet, melt half of the butter over medium heat until bubbling. Add 2 soaked bread slices to the pan. Cook for about 4 minutes, until dark golden brown, then flip and cook on the second side for another 4 minutes, until dark golden brown. Transfer to a plate and repeat with the remaining bread and butter.

SYRUP REQUIRED

♥ SWEET ♥ FRENCH TOAST SANDWICHES

Nutella and Banana French Toast Sandwich *(page 85)*,
Fresh Fruit Custard French Toast Sandwich *(page 84)*,
Banana Custard French Toast Sandwich *(page 82)*

❤ *CRUNCHY FRENCH TOAST*

French toast is delicious, but what is one way to make it even more delicious? Give it a crunchy outside with the classic soft center. It is no secret that I am a big fan of texture and crunch in my food. It is an easy way to elevate your food and take it to the next level.

4 large eggs

2 tablespoons whole milk

⅛ teaspoon ground cinnamon

2 cups cornflakes

4 large (½-inch-thick) slices stale bread (I prefer brioche or challah)

1 tablespoon unsalted butter

1 In a large shallow bowl, whisk together the eggs, milk, and cinnamon.

2 Dump the cornflakes onto a large plate, then crush them into smaller pieces with your hands.

3 Soak the slices of bread in the egg mixture for about 20 seconds on each side.

4 Remove a slice of bread and place it on the plate of cornflakes. Coat both sides of the bread with cornflakes and set aside on a plate (if using for a French toast sandwich, coat only *one* side of the bread slices with cornflakes). Repeat with the remaining bread slices.

5 In a large skillet, melt half of the butter over medium heat until bubbling. Add 2 bread slices (cornflake-side down if using for a French toast sandwich). Cook for 4 minutes, or until the cornflakes begin to turn dark golden brown, then flip and cook on the second side for another 4 minutes, or until the cornflakes begin to turn dark golden brown. Transfer to a plate and repeat with the remaining bread and butter.

SYRUP REQUIRED

♥ BANANA CUSTARD FRENCH TOAST SANDWICH

All right . . . I admit this recipe is a little more laborious than your average French toast. But trust me—it is well worth it! You will even have some banana pudding left over for dessert—just add some wafer cookies and whipped cream. Who could be mad at that?! The custard does need to chill in the fridge for 1 hour, so leave yourself time for that step. You can even make the custard the day before so you can wake up and just enjoy this delicious treat.

1 very ripe banana, plus 1 ripe but firm banana, sliced, for garnish

1 cup whole milk

1 teaspoon vanilla extract

1½ tablespoons sweetened condensed milk

1½ tablespoons unsalted butter, at room temperature

1 tablespoon cornstarch

3 tablespoons sugar

2 egg yolks

1 recipe Crunchy French Toast (page 81)

Warm maple syrup, for serving

1 In a small pot, combine the very ripe banana and the whole milk and break up the banana with a spoon or rubber spatula. Bring the milk to a boil, then remove the pot from the heat. Cover it with plastic wrap or the lid of the pot and set aside for 30 minutes to let the banana infuse the milk.

2 Meanwhile, in a small bowl, combine the vanilla, condensed milk, and butter and set aside.

3 In a separate small bowl, whisk together the cornstarch and 1½ tablespoons of the sugar to combine.

4 Strain the milk through a fine-mesh sieve into a medium bowl, pressing against the banana with a spatula to extract all the milk and then scraping any mashed banana from the outside of the strainer into the bowl. You want to get all that good banana flavor into the milk.

5 Add the remaining 1½ tablespoons sugar to the milk and return the milk to the pot. Bring the milk to a boil. Meanwhile, vigorously whisk the egg yolks into the cornstarch mixture until the mixture is thick and pale yellow in color and forms thick ribbons when you lift out the whisk.

6 Fill a large bowl with ice and a little water and set it nearby.

7 Once the milk begins to boil, while whisking, pour a small amount into the egg yolk mixture and continue whisking until well combined. While whisking continuously, pour the egg yolk–milk mixture back into the pot with the rest of the milk and whisk until the mixture thickens and boils. Cook, whisking continuously, for at least 1 minute, being sure to scrape the bottom and side edges of the pot with the whisk to make sure the mixture doesn't overcook or burn. The key here is to cook it until it really thickens up to the consistency of pudding. If it is too runny, it will spill out of your French toast—not the worst thing in the world, but the thicker, the better (for pudding eating, too).

8 Remove the pot from the heat and stir in the condensed milk mixture.

9 Pour the custard into a small bowl and place the bowl in the ice bath to cool, stirring the custard occasionally. Remove the bowl with the cooled custard from the ice bath, press plastic wrap directly against the surface to prevent condensation from forming and dripping into the custard and making it watery, and refrigerate for at least 1 hour or up to 24 hours to set.

10 Meanwhile, make the Crunchy French Toast.

11 Spread a generous amount of the banana custard over the plain side of one slice of French toast. Arrange half the banana slices on top. Cover with another slice of French toast, with the cornflake-side up, and set the sandwich on a plate. Repeat to make a second sandwich.

12 Top with warm maple syrup and dig in!

❤ *FRESH FRUIT CUSTARD FRENCH TOAST SANDWICH*

This is similar to the Banana Custard French Toast, but with a classic vanilla custard that you can can make ahead and enjoy as a dessert pudding. Add any fresh fruit, peaches, plums, or mango— you get the idea. Like the banana custard, this custard will also need to chill for at least 1 hour to set, so be sure to allow yourself enough time, or make it the day before and refrigerate it overnight.

1 teaspoon vanilla extract

1½ tablespoons unsalted butter, at room temperature

1 tablespoon cornstarch

3 tablespoons granulated sugar

1 cup whole milk

2 egg yolks

1 recipe Crunchy French Toast (page 81)

Fresh berries or fruit of your choice, for serving

Confectioners' sugar, for garnish

Warm maple syrup, for serving

1   In a small bowl, combine the vanilla and butter and set aside.

2   In a separate small bowl, whisk together the cornstarch and 1½ tablespoons of the granulated sugar to combine.

3   In a small pot, combine the milk and remaining 1½ tablespoons granulated sugar and bring the milk to a boil. Meanwhile, vigorously whisk the egg yolks into the cornstarch mixture until the mixture is thick and pale yellow in color and forms thick ribbons when you lift out the whisk.

4   Fill a large bowl with ice and a little water and set it nearby.

5   Once the milk begins to boil, while whisking, pour a small amount into the egg yolk mixture and continue whisking until well combined. While whisking continuously, pour the egg yolk–milk mixture back into the pot with the rest of the milk and whisk until the mixture thickens and boils. Cook, whisking continuously, for 1 minute, being sure to scrape the bottom and side edges of the pot with the whisk to make sure the mixture doesn't overcook or burn. The key here is to cook it until it really thickens up to the consistency of pudding. If it is too runny, it will spill out of your French toast—not the worst thing in the world, but the thicker, the better (for pudding eating, too).

6 Remove the pot from the heat and stir in the vanilla-butter mixture.

7 Pour the custard into a small bowl and place the bowl in the ice bath to cool, stirring the custard occasionally. Remove the bowl with the cooled custard from the ice bath, press plastic wrap directly against the surface of the custard to prevent condensation from forming and dripping into the custard and making it watery, and refrigerate for at least 1 hour or up to 24 hours to set.

8 Meanwhile, make the Crunchy French Toast.

9 Scrape a little bread out of the center of the plain side of a slice of French toast and fill it with a generous amount of custard. Top the custard with lots of fresh berries. Cover with another slice of French toast, with the cornflake-side up, and set the sandwich on a plate. Repeat to make a second sandwich.

10 Dust with confectioners' sugar, slather with maple syrup, and enjoy.

NUTELLA AND BANANA FRENCH TOAST SANDWICH Prepare the Crunchy French Toast. Spread 2 generous tablespoons Nutella on the plain side of one slice of French toast, add some sliced banana, and top with a slice of French toast with the cornflakes on the outside. Dust with confectioners' sugar. YUM!

PB&J FRENCH TOAST SANDWICH Prepare the Crunchy French Toast. Spread 2 tablespoons peanut butter on the plain side of a piece of French toast and 1½ tablespoons of your favorite jelly on another and put the slices together for a sandwich. Top with maple syrup or dust with confectioners' sugar to serve.

◆ SAVORY ◆ FRENCH TOAST SANDWICHES

Turkey, Egg, Spinach, and Swiss French Toast Sandwich,
Eggs Benedict French Toast Sandwich, *from left to right, page 90*

◆ SAVORY FRENCH TOAST

I love a breakfast sandwich and I love French toast, so why
not combine the two?! I was a little skeptical at first, but this
soon became my new favorite breakfast twist.

4 large eggs

2 tablespoons whole milk

Large pinch of fine sea salt

4 (½-inch-thick) slices stale
bread (I prefer brioche
or challah)

1 tablespoon unsalted butter

1 In a large shallow bowl, whisk together the eggs, milk, and salt.

2 Soak the slices of bread in the egg mixture for 30 to 45 seconds on
each side. Set aside on a plate.

3 In a large skillet, melt half of the butter over medium heat until
bubbling. Add 2 soaked bread slices. Cook for 4 minutes, or until
dark golden brown, then flip and cook on the second side for 4 more
minutes, until dark golden brown. Transfer to a plate and repeat with
the remaining bread and butter.

◆ BLT FRENCH TOAST SANDWICH WITH EGG AND SPICY AIOLI

If you haven't noticed, I like to take classics and do 'em up a bit. So this BLT gets the French toast treatment. To me, there is nothing more classic than a BLT, and for breakfast, it doesn't get much more classic than French toast. The spicy aioli can be served on just about anything as well. Drizzle it over sunny-side-up eggs (page 29) or scrambled eggs (page 26) or even add it to the Turkey, Egg, Spinach, and Swiss French Toast Sandwich (page 90)—have fun with it.

SPICY AIOLI

¼ cup mayonnaise

1½ teaspoons sriracha

Squeeze of fresh lemon juice

Large pinch of fine sea salt

Pinch of freshly ground black pepper

SANDWICHES

6 slices bacon

2 large eggs

1 recipe Savory French Toast (page 87—this one works best when the French toast is made with brioche or sourdough)

Fresh arugula

4 slices tomato

1   **To make the spicy aioli:** In a small bowl, stir together all the aioli ingredients. Set aside.

2   **To make the sandwiches:** In a large skillet over high heat, cook bacon approximately 4 minutes per side, or until dark brown and crispy (cooking time for bacon may vary depending on thickness). Set aside cooked bacon on a plate lined with paper towels. In a small skillet, cook the eggs sunny-side up according to the instructions on page 29. At the same time, prepare the Savory French Toast.

3   Spread a generous layer of aioli on one slice of French toast. On top of the aioli, layer arugula, 2 tomato slices, 1 egg, and 3 slices of bacon. Top with another slice of French toast and set the sandwich on a plate. Repeat to make a second sandwich, and enjoy.

recipe continues

TURKEY, EGG, SPINACH, AND SWISS FRENCH TOAST SANDWICH

Preheat the oven to 200°F. Prepare the Savory French Toast. Once cooked, place on a baking sheet in the oven. Place a slice of cheese on one slice of French toast to melt in the oven while keeping the French toast warm. Cook the eggs sunny-side up according to the instructions on page 29. Once the eggs are cooked, push them over to the side of the pan and add the turkey slices to the pan to heat them. Remove the French toast from the oven to build your sandwich. Spread mustard on the piece of French toast without cheese, add an egg on top of the French toast with cheese, add turkey slices and spinach. Top with remaining French toast with mustard. Repeat to make second sandwich and enjoy.

EGGS BENEDICT FRENCH TOAST SANDWICH

Cook the eggs sunny-side up according to the instructions on page 29. While the eggs are cooking, prepare the Savory French Toast. Apply a generous amount of hollandaise sauce (page 47) to the French toast slices. Layer 2 slices ham and 1 sunny-side-up egg on a piece of French toast. Top with another slice of French toast. Repeat to make a second sandwich.

◆ ALMOND FRANGIPANE AND PEAR BAKED FRENCH TOAST

This is one of those weird creations that came to me out of nowhere, a vision, if you will. I imagined the finished product first, then I brainstormed the best way to execute it. I had no idea how it would turn out, but boy oh boy, am I glad I experimented and got creative!

FRANGIPANE

2 tablespoons all-purpose flour

¼ cup sugar

½ cup slivered almonds

Pinch of fine sea salt

3 tablespoons unsalted butter, at room temperature

1 large egg

½ teaspoon vanilla extract

⅛ teaspoon almond extract

1 teaspoon bourbon

FRENCH TOAST

Butter or nonstick cooking spray, for the pan

6 (¾- to 1-inch-thick) slices brioche or challah, left out overnight to get stale

3 tablespoons unsalted butter, melted

6 large eggs

1 cup whole milk

1 teaspoon vanilla extract

Pinch of fine sea salt

1 or 2 Bartlett or Anjou pears

Sliced almonds, for sprinkling

Confectioners' sugar, for sprinkling

1 **To make the frangipane:** In a food processor, combine the flour, sugar, almonds, and salt and pulse until the almonds are finely ground. Add the butter and pulse until smooth. Add the egg, vanilla, almond extract, and bourbon. Pulse until smooth and combined.

2 **To make the French toast:** Preheat the oven to 400°F. Line a baking sheet with parchment paper. Lightly grease a 9 by 5-inch loaf pan with butter or nonstick spray.

3 Brush both sides of each bread slice with the melted butter and place them on the prepared baking sheet. Toast the bread in the oven until golden brown. Remove from the oven and let the toast cool.

4 In a medium bowl, whisk together the eggs, milk, vanilla, and salt until well combined. Pour the egg mixture into a shallow dish or container.

5 Soak the toasted bread slices in the egg mixture for about 15 minutes on each side. Set aside in a dish.

recipe continues

6   While the bread is soaking, peel the pears. Slice the pears from top to bottom into ⅛- to ¼-inch-thick slices, removing the seeds from the center. You want whole pear pieces.

7   Spread about 2 tablespoons of the frangipane over a soaked bread slice and place the bread upright at the end of the prepared loaf pan. Next to that, add a pear slice. Repeat this order until done, ending with a pear slice. Sprinkle the top with sliced almonds.

8   Bake for 45 to 50 minutes, until the bread is springy and the center of the frangipane is fluffy. Remove from the oven, let it cool slightly, sprinkle with confectioners' sugar, then slice and serve immediately.

FANCY FILLING

Frangipane is just a fancy word for an almond filling used in tarts, croissants, and other breakfast pastries and desserts.

BISCUITS, MUFFINS, BREADS

& MORE BAKED GOODIES

BUTTERMILK BISCUITS

Not much needs to be said about biscuits . . . other than that they are *amazing*. And not so great for the waistline. But everything in moderation, right? Yes, these use a whole stick of butter, and that is why they are so good.

1½ cups all-purpose flour

1 tablespoon sugar

2 teaspoons baking powder

¼ teaspoon baking soda

½ teaspoon fine sea salt

½ cup (1 stick) unsalted butter, cubed and chilled

½ cup cold buttermilk

1 large egg, beaten

1   Preheat the oven to 450°F. Line a baking sheet with parchment paper or a silicone baking mat.

2   In a large bowl, combine the flour, sugar, baking powder, baking soda, and salt. Stir together with a fork. Using the large holes of a cheese grater, grate the butter into the flour. A quarter of the way through grating, stop and gently toss the butter pieces into the flour to coat. Repeat every quarter of the way until done.

3   Make a well in the center of the flour mixture and pour in the buttermilk. Gently mix with a fork—do not overmix or handle the dough too roughly (the key to great biscuits is in the gentle handling of the dough). The dough may still seem dry in spots but should come together. If needed, you can add an additional tablespoon or two of buttermilk.

4   Turn it out onto a floured surface and gently fold it over on itself a few times. Pat the dough out to about 1 inch thick, then gently loosen it from the work surface and almost shake it out a bit. (This is my trick for any dough recipe—after you have rolled it out, you want to relax the gluten and loosen it back up a bit. Think of it as jiggling or shaking out your muscles after a massage or workout.)

5   With a 2- or 3-inch round cookie cutter, cut out biscuits and place them on the prepared baking sheet. (Alternatively, you can pull off balls of dough and place them on the baking sheet. They don't have to

recipe continues

be perfect—the more rustic looking, the better.) See note (page 99) for using a cast-iron skillet.

6   Brush the biscuits with the beaten egg. Bake for 15 minutes or until golden brown, rotating the baking sheet halfway through the cooking time. Best served warm from the oven. To store extras, keep in a sealed container at room temperature. To reheat, bake in the oven at 300°F for 5 minutes.

ROSEMARY BISCUITS Add 2 tablespoons finely chopped fresh rosemary to the dry ingredients and proceed as directed.

PREP TIME: 1 minute   **TOTAL TIME:** 2 minutes   **YIELD:** Makes ½ cup

HONEY BUTTER

How can you possibly improve on a buttery biscuit? Spread even more butter and honey all over it! It's magic.

½ cup (1 stick) unsalted butter, at room temperature

2 tablespoons honey

Pinch of fine sea salt

In the bowl of a stand mixer fitted with the paddle attachment (or in a large bowl using a handheld mixer), beat the butter on medium to high speed until soft and fluffy. Add the honey and salt and beat to combine.

Rosemary Biscuits, *opposite*

TO BAKE BISCUITS IN A CAST-IRON SKILLET

Preheat the oven to 450°F. Generously grease the bottom and sides of a 12-inch cast-iron skillet. Evenly space and arrange the biscuits in the skillet. Brush with egg wash and bake approximately 15 minutes until lightly golden brown, rotating the skillet halfway through baking.

BACON-CHEDDAR BISCUITS

I love biscuits. I love them in the morning, I love them for lunch, I love them for dinner. They are an all-around winner. So why not make a biscuit that's almost a meal in itself? That idea was my inspiration for these rich, cheesy, bacon-y biscuits. Perfect to eat on their own or as a great accompaniment for breakfast, lunch, or dinner.

2 cups all-purpose flour

4 teaspoons baking powder

¼ teaspoon baking soda

1 teaspoon fine sea salt

6 tablespoons (¾ stick) unsalted butter, cubed and chilled

1 cup buttermilk, plus more for topping

½ cup chopped cooked bacon

¼ cup plus 2 tablespoons shredded sharp Cheddar cheese, plus more for topping

Maldon sea salt, for topping

1 Preheat the oven to 450°F. Line a baking sheet with parchment paper or a silicone baking mat.

2 In a large bowl, combine the flour, baking powder, baking soda, and fine sea salt. Stir together with a fork.

3 Using the large holes of a cheese grater, grate the butter into the flour. A quarter of the way through grating, stop and gently toss the butter pieces into the flour to coat. Repeat every quarter of the way until done.

4 Make a well in the center of the flour mixture and pour in the buttermilk. Gently mix with a fork—do not overmix or handle too roughly (the key to great biscuits is in the gentle handling of the dough). Just before the buttermilk is completely mixed in, add the bacon and cheese.

5 The dough may still seem dry in spots. Turn it out onto a floured surface and gently fold it over on itself a few times. Pat the dough out to about 1 inch thick, then gently loosen it from the work surface and almost shake it out a bit. (This is my trick for any dough recipe—after you have rolled it out, you want to relax the gluten and loosen it back up a bit. Think of it as jiggling or shaking out your muscles after a massage or workout.)

6 Cut out rounds using a 3-inch round cookie cutter. (Alternatively, you can pull off balls of dough instead of using a cutter. They don't have to be perfect—the more rustic looking the better.)

7 Place biscuits an inch or so apart on the prepared baking sheet. Combine the dough scraps, being careful to handle the dough gently, pat them out to 1 inch thick, and cut out more biscuits. Repeat until no usable dough remains.

8 Brush the tops with a little buttermilk, then sprinkle the cheese and a pinch of Maldon sea salt on top of each biscuit. Bake for 10 to 15 minutes, until very light golden brown, rotating the baking sheet halfway through the cooking time.

RASPBERRY CITRUS WHOLE WHEAT MUFFINS

I love whole wheat baked goods, but I see how they aren't for everyone as the whole wheat gives them a more wholesome and healthy taste. Adding the raspberry and citrus to this muffin really brightens it up and balances the earthy heartiness of whole wheat—leaving you with a more nutritious but still delicious muffin.

¾ cup whole wheat flour

½ cup sugar, plus more for sprinkling

¾ teaspoon baking powder

¼ teaspoon baking soda

¼ teaspoon fine sea salt

1 teaspoon orange zest

1 large egg, beaten

¼ cup whole milk

¼ cup vegetable oil or canola oil

1 teaspoon vanilla extract

¾ cup fresh raspberries

1   Preheat the oven to 375°F. Grease eight wells of a muffin tin or line them with paper liners.

2   In a large bowl, whisk together the flour, sugar, baking powder, baking soda, salt, and orange zest.

3   In a small bowl, stir together the egg, milk, oil, and vanilla.

4   Add the raspberries to the flour mixture. Add the egg mixture to the flour mixture and stir to combine.

5   Fill the prepared muffin cups three-quarters full with the batter. Sprinkle the tops with sugar. Bake for 15 to 20 minutes, until the muffins are golden brown on top and spring back when lightly touched in the center.

BLUEBERRY–EARL GREY MUFFINS

I always like to find ways to add another layer of flavor to make things a bit more complex, or just more fun. Adding tea to baked goods has been one of my favorite ways to do just that, ever since my culinary school days. The classic muffin gets a fun makeover (and a little caffeine buzz) from Earl Grey tea.

1 cup all-purpose flour

½ cup sugar, plus more for sprinkling

¾ teaspoon baking powder

¼ teaspoon baking soda

Pinch of lemon zest

¼ teaspoon fine sea salt

1 Earl Grey tea bag

1 large egg, beaten

¼ cup whole milk

1 teaspoon vanilla extract

¼ cup vegetable oil or canola oil

¾ cup fresh blueberries

1   Preheat the oven to 375°F. Grease eight wells of a muffin tin or line them with paper liners.

2   In a large bowl, combine the flour, sugar, baking powder, baking soda, lemon zest, and salt. Cut open the tea bag and add the tea leaves to the dry ingredients. Whisk together.

3   In a small bowl, stir together the egg, milk, vanilla, and oil.

4   Add the blueberries to the flour mixture. Add the egg mixture to the flour mixture and stir to combine.

5   Fill the prepared muffin cups three-quarters full with the batter. Sprinkle the tops with sugar. Bake for 15 to 20 minutes, until the muffins are golden brown on top and spring back when lightly touched in the center.

Honey–Cranberry Bran Muffin, *opposite*

Pumpkin–Cream Cheese Muffin, *page 108*

HONEY-CRANBERRY BRAN MUFFINS

MUFFINS

⅔ cup packed brown sugar

¼ cup honey

¼ cup plus 1 tablespoon vegetable oil or canola oil

1 large egg

1½ cups buttermilk

¼ teaspoon firmly packed orange zest

2 teaspoons molasses

1 teaspoon vanilla extract

1 cup all-purpose flour

2 cups wheat bran

¾ teaspoon baking soda

½ teaspoon fine sea salt

½ cup dried cranberries, unsweetened

HONEY GLAZE

2 tablespoons unsalted butter, at room temperature

¼ cup honey

3 tablespoons brown sugar

Small pinch of fine sea salt

I love a bran muffin, but let's be real—bran is dry and has a thick flake and texture, so in order to make it more delicious, we add sugar or fruit. Here I have added both. The glaze sits in the muffin cup and bakes into the muffin, making it moist and sweet.

1 Preheat the oven to 375°F.

2 **To make the muffins:** In the bowl of a stand mixer fitted with the paddle attachment, combine the brown sugar and honey and mix until smooth. Add the oil and egg, then mix until combined and smooth. Add the buttermilk, orange zest, molasses, and vanilla. Beat until combined.

3 In a medium bowl, stir together the flour, bran, baking soda, salt, and cranberries. Slowly add the dry ingredients to the wet and mix until combined.

4 **To make the honey glaze:** In the bowl of a standard mixer fitted with a paddle attachment, or with a hand mixer, cream together the butter, honey, brown sugar, and salt until smooth. Evenly distribute the glaze among the cups of a 12-well muffin pan, putting 1 to 2 teaspoons in each cup. Spread the glaze over the bottom and about halfway up the sides of each cup.

5 Fill the muffin cups a little over three-quarters full with the batter. Bake for 20 minutes, until the muffins are lightly golden brown and spring back when lightly touched in the center.

6 Remove the muffins from the oven and immediately invert the muffin pan onto a baking sheet or a sheet of foil. Let the muffins cool and enjoy. Store in an airtight container at room temperature.

LEMON-POPPY SEED MUFFINS

This is a classic muffin, and one of my favorites. I love the crunchy
little poppy seeds with the bright citrus flavor—a perfect wake-you-
up breakfast muffin.

1 cup all-purpose flour

½ cup sugar, plus more for
sprinkling

¾ teaspoon baking powder

¼ teaspoon baking soda

¼ teaspoon fine sea salt

Zest of 1 lemon

1 teaspoon orange zest

2 teaspoons poppy seeds

1 large egg, beaten

¼ cup whole milk

1 teaspoon vanilla extract

¼ cup vegetable oil or canola oil

Juice of 1 lemon

1   Preheat the oven to 375°F. Grease eight wells of a muffin tin or line
them with paper liners.

2   In a large bowl, whisk together the flour, sugar, baking powder,
baking soda, salt, lemon zest, orange zest, and poppy seeds until
combined.

3   In a small bowl, combine the egg, milk, vanilla, and oil. Stir to
combine. Add the lemon juice and stir. Add the egg mixture to the
flour mixture, stirring to combine.

4   Fill the prepared wells of the muffin tin three-quarters full with the
batter. Sprinkle the tops with sugar. Bake for 15 to 20 minutes, until
the muffins are golden brown on top and spring back when lightly
touched in the center.

PREP TIME: 5 minutes   **TOTAL TIME:** 20 to 25 minutes   **YIELD:** Makes 8 muffins

BANANA MOCHA CHOCOLATE CHIP MUFFINS

These muffins were a staple at my very first restaurant in Costa Rica. Surfers would pass through on their way to the beach and grab one for surf fuel. Everybody walked around in bathing suits carrying surfboards, so with no place for a wallet, everybody in town had an open tab running. Small towns use the honor system like that, and I loved it! Feel free to have fun with these and add butterscotch or peanut butter chips instead of the chocolate chips.

3 bananas, the riper, the better

1 cup all-purpose flour

½ cup sugar, plus more for sprinkling

¾ teaspoon baking powder

¼ teaspoon baking soda

¼ teaspoon ground cinnamon

⅛ teaspoon ground nutmeg

¼ teaspoon fine sea salt

1 teaspoon instant espresso powder (I prefer Medaglia d'Oro; optional)

½ cup chocolate chips

¼ cup chopped walnuts

1 large egg, beaten

¼ cup vegetable oil or canola oil

1 teaspoon vanilla extract

1 Preheat the oven to 375°F. Grease eight wells of a muffin tin or line them with paper liners.

2 In a small or medium bowl, mash the bananas with a fork or potato masher and set aside.

3 In a large bowl, whisk together the flour, sugar, baking powder, baking soda, cinnamon, nutmeg, salt, and espresso powder (if using) until combined. Add the chocolate chips and walnuts and stir to combine.

4 In a small bowl, stir together the egg, oil, and vanilla. Add the banana and stir to combine. Add the egg mixture to the flour mixture and stir to combine.

5 Fill the prepared muffin cups three-quarters full with the batter. Sprinkle the tops with sugar. Bake for 15 to 20 minutes, until the muffins are golden brown on top and spring back when lightly touched in the center.

BISCUITS, MUFFINS, BREADS & MORE BAKED GOODIES

PUMPKIN–CREAM CHEESE MUFFINS

Oh, pumpkin and cream cheese, how I love ya! This perfect partnership will have you yearning for pumpkin season all year long. Thank goodness you can buy canned pumpkin at the market any day of the year.

MUFFINS

1 cup all-purpose flour

½ cup granulated sugar

¾ teaspoon baking powder

¼ teaspoon baking soda

¾ teaspoon ground cinnamon

¼ teaspoon fine sea salt

1 large egg, beaten

¼ cup vegetable oil or canola oil

¼ cup whole milk

½ cup plus 2 tablespoons canned pure pumpkin purée

1 teaspoon vanilla extract

CREAM CHEESE FILLING

½ (8-ounce) package cream cheese, at room temperature

2 tablespoons granulated sugar

STREUSEL TOPPING

1 tablespoon unsalted butter, cubed and chilled

¼ teaspoon fine sea salt

3 tablespoons all-purpose flour

3 tablespoons brown sugar

¼ cup finely chopped pecans

¼ teaspoon ground cinnamon

1 Preheat the oven to 375°F. Grease ten wells of a muffin tin or line them with paper liners.

2 **To make the muffins:** In a large bowl, whisk together the flour, granulated sugar, baking powder, baking soda, cinnamon, and salt to combine.

3 In a medium bowl, stir together the egg, oil, milk, pumpkin, and vanilla. Add the egg mixture to the flour mixture and stir to combine.

4 **To make the cream cheese filling:** In the bowl of a stand mixer fitted with the paddle attachment (or in a large bowl using a handheld mixer), beat together the cream cheese and granulated sugar until combined.

5 **To make the streusel topping:** In a small bowl, stir together the butter, salt, flour, brown sugar, pecans, and cinnamon. Using your fingers or a fork, mix until the butter is broken down into small pea-size pieces.

6 Fill the prepared muffin cups one-third full with the batter. Place about 1 teaspoon of the cream cheese mixture in the very center of the batter in each cup and push it down slightly. Add more batter to each muffin cup to fill them three-quarters full. Top each with 1 tablespoon of the streusel. Bake for about 20 minutes, or until the streusel is golden brown on top and the muffins spring back when lightly touched in the center.

BAGUETTE

This is the ultimate recipe to show off what a fancy pants you are in the kitchen . . . even if you aren't. I truly believe everything homemade is better, but bread is where you taste it the most. So there is no excuse not to make your own fresh French baguette, crispy crunchy on the outside and soft and airy on the inside. Trust me, it's doable for every home baker and cook. Sure, the entire process takes 15 to 18 hours, but the actual hands-on time is nothing, and it is *sooo* worth it. Eat it on its own with cheese, toast it with butter and jam, use it for bruschetta, take it to a dinner party—basically, you can't go wrong.

There are a few different ways to make a baguette—you can go sourdough or classic, fast or slow. This recipe may take longer than others, but I tried them all and this one reigns supreme. It gives you a better crust, crumb, and flavor. Your patience will be rewarded.

POOLISH STARTER

1½ cups all-purpose flour

¾ teaspoon active dry yeast

1 cup plus 2 tablespoons warm water

BAGUETTE

1½ cups all-purpose flour

¼ cup warm water

1½ teaspoons fine sea salt

1 **To make the poolish starter:** In a medium to large bowl (large enough that the starter will have room to grow), combine the flour, yeast, and warm water. With a large whisk, vigorously mix until the dough becomes sticky and stringy and bubbles begin to form. Cover the bowl with plastic wrap. Write the time on the plastic and set the dough aside at room temperature (or a little bit warmer, if possible) to rise, undisturbed, for 12 to 14 hours. The starter will bubble and grow.

2 **To make the baguette:** In the bowl of a stand mixer fitted with the dough hook, combine the poolish starter, flour, warm water, and salt. Mix on medium speed for 5 to 8 minutes, stopping every now and then in the beginning to scrape the bottom and sides of the bowl, until the dough comes together in a ball and is shiny. The dough should not rip easily when pulled—it should have good elasticity. It should not be too sticky, either. (See Note, page 112.)

recipe continues

If the dough feels too sticky, add 1 tablespoon flour until it reaches the correct consistency. Alternatively, if the dough is too dry, you can add 1 tablespoon water. Always be sure to add very small amounts of flour and water at a time to get the correct consistency and allow it to mix for a minute or two before adding more. When you're making bread dough, it can be very finicky depending on the humidity, temperature, and other factors, so you may have to adjust the amount of flour and water a little bit.

POOLISH WHAT?

So bread is a crazy art and science, and there is so much involved that it would take an entire other book to get into it. I have so much respect for bread, its process, and its bakers. It can take a lifetime to master bread, and I don't claim to be an expert. So this is the CliffsNotes version on one option of a bread starter. This is a pre-ferment bread starter. It is a combination of flour, water, and yeast allowed to ferment and then added to dough to act as the leavening agent, the yeast, in the dough. Some recipes will also add more yeast, but it just depends. By creating this starter and allowing it to ferment, you get more flavor in your dough. You are allowing the yeast to grow and ferment, basically to get funky to add flavor and to add leavening to your finished product. It is more labor-intensive and takes much more time than just adding straight active yeast, but the results pay off in the end. You get better taste and better texture. All good things come to those who wait.

3   Turn the dough out onto a lightly floured surface and fold it over on itself six to eight times, until it feels tight. Form the dough into a ball and place it in a lightly floured or greased bowl. Loosely cover the bowl with plastic wrap and write the time on the plastic. (This step is important, as it lets you know exactly when the dough was made so you know exactly how long it has been resting.) Set the dough aside at room temperature (or slightly warmer) to rise for 1 hour.

4   Turn the dough out onto a lightly floured surface. Flatten and deflate the dough, shape it into a ball, return it to the bowl, cover, and set aside to rest for 1 hour more.

5   Turn the dough out onto a lightly floured surface, flatten and deflate it, and cut it in half. Flatten each half into a rectangle. From the bottom, fold the dough upward a little over halfway up and flatten it with the heel of your hand. Repeat once or twice, until you have a log shape. Set the dough seam-side down on your work surface, lightly dust the top with flour, and loosely cover it with plastic wrap. Repeat with the second rectangle of dough and let both rest for 20 minutes.

6   Carefully turn one rectangle of dough over so it's seam-side up and, much more gently this time, fold the top up and flatten it with the heel of your hand. Repeat once. Set the dough seam-side down on your work surface and evenly roll it out to about 15 inches long, trying to get the ends pointy like a baguette. Dust a baguette pan with flour and gently set the dough in one well. (If you don't have a baguette pan, shape long folds into a kitchen towel and generously flour the folds to hold the baguettes.) Repeat with the second rectangle of dough and set it in the pan.

7   Lightly spray the tops of the baguettes with water to keep them moist. Set the baguettes aside to proof (I generally do this next to the oven for the warmth; for more on proofing, see page 148). Proof the baguettes for 20 to 40 minutes, depending on the temperature of your kitchen, until the dough has plumped up—do not allow it to double in size. Spray the baguettes with water as necessary to ensure the dough does not dry out (you don't want the dough wet, just moist—this will help it rise).

recipe continues

step 5

step 6

step 6

step 9

8 While the baguettes proof, place a pot filled with water on the bottom rack in the oven and preheat the oven to 500ºF.

9 If you have a baking stone, you can use that for the next steps. Otherwise, take a large baking sheet, flip it upside down, and line it with parchment paper or a silicone baking mat (see Note). Very gently roll the baguettes seam-side down onto the stone or baking sheet. With a very sharp knife or baker's blade, gently make three shallow cuts, about 3 inches long, at an equal distance apart, down the top of each baguette. You don't want to cut too deep, just enough to break the surface.

10 Place the baguettes, still on the stone or baking sheet, in the oven on the top rack. With a water bottle, spray a generous amount of water inside the oven and close the door. Bake for 13 minutes, opening the oven door every 4 minutes and spraying some water inside. Reduce the oven temperature to 450ºF and bake for 12 to 18 minutes, until the baguettes are golden brown, rotating the stone or baking sheet halfway through the cooking time. Let the baguettes cool slightly, but it is best to enjoy while still warm from the oven. To store, wrap tightly in plastic wrap and keep at room temp. Baguettes are best fresh, day of, but if kept wrapped can be stored for 2 days.

BRIOCHE

Brioche is one of my favorite breads to use for French toast, bread pudding, etc., because it is soft, rich, and buttery. The spectrum of how much butter to use in brioche varies greatly. I've seen recipes that are basically 100 percent butter. This one is a good all-purpose brioche recipe. Feel free to add a few more tablespoons of butter if you like, but this recipe won't disappoint as is.

3 cups all-purpose flour

1 teaspoon fine sea salt

4 tablespoons sugar

⅓ cup warm milk

2½ teaspoons active dry yeast

4 large eggs, plus 1 egg beaten with a splash of water for egg wash

1 cup (2 sticks) unsalted butter, cubed and chilled

1   In the bowl of a stand mixer fitted with the dough hook, stir together the flour, salt, and sugar by hand.

2   Put the warm milk in a small bowl or measuring cup, add the yeast, and stir to dissolve.

3   With the stand mixer on low speed, add the milk-yeast mixture to the flour mixture. Increase the speed to medium-low and mix for 30 seconds or so, then lower the speed and add the 4 eggs, one at a time. Mix on medium to high speed until the dough comes together into a ball and is smooth, 5 minutes or more.

4   Slowly add the butter and mix on medium to high speed, stopping occasionally to scrape the bottom of the bowl, until the dough is smooth and elastic. The dough should not break apart easily when you pull it apart—it should come together into a smooth ball. After you add the butter, the mixing time may take 10 to 15 minutes.

5   Turn out the dough onto a lightly floured surface. Fold the dough over on itself a few times, shape it into a ball, and place it in a buttered bowl. Cover the bowl with plastic wrap and set aside for 1 hour, until the dough has doubled in size.

recipe continues

BISCUITS, MUFFINS, BREADS & MORE BAKED GOODIES

6   Use your fingers to gently lift the edges of the dough to deflate it. Cover the bowl and refrigerate for 4 to 6 hours, or up to overnight.

7   Preheat the oven to 375°F. Butter two 9 by 5-inch loaf pans.

8   Turn the dough out onto a lightly floured surface and cut it in half, then cut each half into three equal pieces. (If you have a scale to check that they are equal, that is ideal, but not necessary.) Gently roll each piece into a log shape. Loosely cover the logs with plastic wrap and let them rest for 20 minutes.

9   Roll each log into a rope about 12 inches long.

10   Pinch the tops of 3 ropes together and braid them, then pinch the ends together. Tuck the ends under the braid gently and place the braid in one of the prepared loaf pans.

11   Repeat with the other 3 ropes and place them in the second prepared loaf pan.

12   Brush the top of the loaves with the egg wash and bake for 40 to 45 minutes, until golden brown. Cover the loaves with foil for the last 15 minutes of the baking if the tops are getting too dark.

13   The perfect way to determine if any bread is finished baking is to turn the loaves out onto a rack and tap them on the bottom—each loaf should sound hollow when it's ready. Store loaves wrapped in foil at room temperature.

step 5

step 9

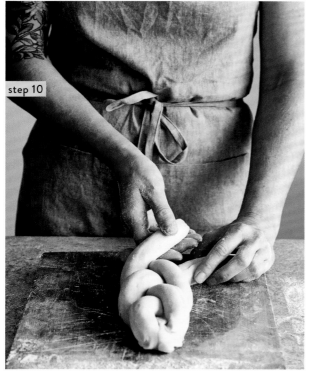

step 10

step 10

GREEK YOGURT–RASPBERRY LOAF

This is a super-moist, almost cake-like or coffee cake–like breakfast loaf. A fruity, moist, tangy, sweet, anytime snack that's perfect with your morning coffee or afternoon tea.

Nonstick cooking spray

1½ cups all-purpose flour

¾ cup granulated sugar

1½ teaspoons baking powder

½ teaspoon fine sea salt

2 large eggs

½ cup coconut oil, melted

1¼ cups full-fat Greek yogurt

1 cup raspberries

½ teaspoon lemon zest

Coarse sugar, for sprinkling

1 Preheat the oven to 350ºF. Grease a 9 by 5-inch loaf pan.

2 In the bowl of a stand mixer fitted with the whisk attachment, combine the flour, granulated sugar, baking powder, and salt. Mix well on low speed. Add the eggs and coconut oil and mix until just combined. Add the yogurt and mix until just combined. Add the raspberries and lemon zest. Gently mix just to distribute the raspberries. Don't overmix—you don't want to smash the raspberries too much (but a little smashing is okay).

3 Pour the batter into the prepared loaf pan, spreading it evenly with a spatula, and sprinkle the top with coarse sugar. Bake for 40 to 45 minutes, until golden brown and the center springs back when touched. Cover it with foil for the last 15 minutes of baking if the top is getting too brown. Store wrapped in foil at room temperature.

BISCUITS, MUFFINS, BREADS & MORE BAKED GOODIES

GINGERBREAD WITH MOLASSES GLAZE

GINGERBREAD

Nonstick cooking spray

¾ cup molasses

½ cup hot water

¾ cup packed brown sugar

2 large eggs

10 tablespoons (1¼ sticks) unsalted butter, melted

2 cups all-purpose flour

1 tablespoon ground ginger

2 teaspoons ground cloves

1 teaspoon ground cinnamon

2 teaspoons baking soda

1 teaspoon instant espresso powder (I prefer Medaglia d'Oro)

½ teaspoon fine sea salt

MOLASSES GLAZE

1½ cups confectioners' sugar, sifted

¾ teaspoon ground cinnamon

¾ teaspoon ground ginger

3 tablespoons molasses

4 to 5 tablespoons cold water

This gingerbread is deep and dark, filled with great molasses flavor and lots of ginger spice. The glaze adds the perfect zing and sweetness. Divine with coffee for breakfast! And no holiday season is complete without this treat. I always make a few gingerbreads and eat them all day during the month of December.

1   **To make the gingerbread:** Preheat the oven to 350°F. Grease a 9 by 11-inch or similar size baking dish with cooking spray.

2   In the bowl of a stand mixer fitted with the paddle attachment, combine the molasses, hot water, and brown sugar and mix until the batter is smooth and lighter in color. Add the eggs one at a time and mix until incorporated. Add the melted butter and mix to combine.

3   In a large bowl, stir together the flour, ginger, cloves, cinnamon, baking soda, espresso powder, and salt. Slowly add the dry ingredients to the batter and beat on medium-high speed until well combined and fluffy.

4   Pour the batter into the prepared baking dish. Bake for 35 to 40 minutes, until the center springs back when touched.

5   Let the gingerbread cool slightly. Place a sheet of plastic wrap on the counter and set a wire rack on top. Unmold the gingerbread onto the rack and set it right-side up. Let cool until just slightly warm.

6 ***To make the molasses glaze:*** In a medium bowl, stir together the confectioners' sugar, cinnamon, ginger, molasses, and cold water. The glaze should be thin but not too watery—it should have a syrupy consistency. If it's too thin, stir in a little more confectioners' sugar. Make the glaze just before using it (if you need to make it ahead, press a sheet of plastic wrap directly against the surface of the glaze to prevent it from drying out or forming a crust on top).

7 Pour the glaze evenly over the top of the warm gingerbread and let it spill down the sides. Store covered with foil at room temperature.

CARDAMOM BANANA BREAD

This no-frills recipe is delicious, always moist, and super banana-y in flavor. Feel free to add raisins, chocolate chips, or, my favorite, walnuts. I realize there is a forever battle between nuts and no nuts when it comes to banana bread, but I am squarely on the team of nuts! They add flavor and the perfect texture, but of course you can choose the other team, if you must.

Letting your bananas get super, super ripe—like, I'm talking black—is the key to this recipe. If you want to go for a more classic banana bread flavor, omit the cardamom and ginger and add ½ teaspoon ground cinnamon, ¼ teaspoon ground nutmeg, and a pinch of ground cloves.

Nonstick cooking spray

2 cups all-purpose flour

1½ teaspoons baking soda

½ teaspoon ground cardamom

¼ teaspoon ground ginger

½ teaspoon fine sea salt

2 large eggs, at room temperature

2 cups mashed super, super–ripe bananas (about 6 bananas)

1 cup sugar

¾ cup coconut oil, melted

¼ cup chopped walnuts, chocolate chips, or raisins (optional)

1 Preheat the oven to 350°F. Grease a 9 by 5-inch loaf pan.

2 In a large bowl, combine the flour, baking soda, cardamom, ginger, and salt.

3 In a medium bowl, stir together the eggs, bananas, sugar, and coconut oil. Add the banana mixture to the dry ingredients and stir to combine. Add the walnuts (if using) and stir to combine.

4 Pour the batter into the prepared pan, making sure the center is not piled too high. Spread the batter into the corners so it is evenly distributed in the pan.

5 Bake for 30 minutes, then cover the bread with foil so the top doesn't get too brown and bake for 15 to 20 minutes more, until the center springs back when lightly touched or a toothpick inserted into the center comes out clean. Store wrapped in foil at room temperature.

PEACH-THYME JAM

I had a bunch of leftover almost-rotten peaches in my kitchen one day and thought, *What better thing to do with almost-bad overly ripe fruit than make some jam?* When I make jam (and eat jam), I like it fresh and not overly sweet. I also like chunks of real fruit in there, something that reminds me I am in fact eating natural and delicious fruit—not some sweet, super-gelatinized, tooth-hurting, mass-produced syrup that leaves me wondering if it really even started with whole pieces of fruit in the first place. In my quest to always add a bit of edge and create a nice balance of flavors, I thought honey and thyme would be just the thing to add to the peaches. I gave out a few jars to friends the first time I made it, and when the requests started piling in afterward, I added it to my regular repertoire. I even ended up making 130 cute little jars of it to pass out as party favors. I also provide canning instructions with this recipe, should you want to preserve the flavors for a season.

12 to 14 ripe peaches, pitted and chopped (do not peel)

About ⅔ cup honey

2 cups sugar

½ cup fresh orange juice

10 sprigs thyme

1   In a large bowl, stir together all the ingredients. Transfer the mixture to a large pot and bring to a boil over medium to high heat. Reduce the heat to low, cover, and simmer for 2 to 4 hours, checking on the pot occasionally and stirring to keep anything from scorching on the bottom.

2   After about 1 hour 30 minutes, or once the peaches have broken down and become very soft, use a potato masher to mash them up inside the pot. Cook, mash the peaches again every once in a while as they soften further, until the mixture has thickened and become slightly shiny (see Note, page 127).

3   Let the jam cool slightly, then transfer it to mason jars or any airtight container you prefer. It will keep in the fridge for up to 2 weeks. For longer storage, can the jam as directed (see page 127).

recipe continues

BISCUITS, MUFFINS, BREADS & MORE BAKED GOODIES

125

NOTE A trick to help determine when the jam is done is to chill a small plate in the fridge or freezer. Pull it out when you want to check the jam's progress and place a small spoonful of jam on it. The jam will cool and set up quickly on the cold plate, which will give you a good idea of its consistency. We are looking for a jam-like consistency . . . duh. What I mean is this recipe will not yield super-gelatinized jam like you get in the supermarket. Instead, the texture will be thick, shiny, sticky, and slightly chunky, somewhat like a compote, but still spreadable. I prefer mine more natural, which is why I don't use pectin or an obscene amount of sugar.

TO CAN THE JAM

Sterilize your mason jars and rings. Bring a large pot of water to a boil, add the jars and rings, and boil for 5 minutes. (If your dishwasher has a feature for sterilizing, you can sterilize the jars in the dishwasher.) Remove the jars using kitchen tongs or canning tongs and place them on a clean kitchen towel on your counter. (The towel is important, as you don't want to place hot glass jars on a cold counter, which could cause them to break.) The lids should not be boiled; clean them thoroughly and place them in a bowl of warm water to keep the rubber seals soft for a good seal.

Using a funnel or (very carefully) a spoon, fill the jars with jam, leaving ¼ inch of headspace from the top. Be careful not to spill jam on the edges or outside of the jar, which can allow bacteria to grow outside the seal. Once all the jars are filled, wipe the edges and clean up any spills. Use a clean skewer to pop any air bubbles (you can also gently tap the jars against the counter to pop any bubbles).

Remove the lids from the warm water one at a time, shake off excess water, set the rings on the jars, and screw on the rings. (It is best to use a canning magnet tool so you are not touching the lids too much or otherwise contaminating them. If you don't have such a tool, just be careful not to touch the underside of the lid.)

Once all the jars of jam are assembled and sealed, it's time to boil them. Fill a canning pot lined with a rack or a large pot with water and bring to a boil. Place the jars of jam carefully into the boiling water, leaving some space between each jar—you don't want to overcrowd the pot. There should be 1 to 2 inches of water covering the jars. I always have an additional pot of boiling water on the stove to add as needed to keep the jars covered. Return the water to a rolling boil, then set your timer for 10 minutes.

Using tongs, remove the jars from the boiling water and set them on a clean kitchen towel on the counter to cool—don't touch them! You will start to hear the lids popping as they cool. This lets you know the process is working its magic and you have a proper seal. Repeat to can the remaining jars. Let sit untouched on the towel on the counter for 24 hours.

Check all the seals: If the middle doesn't pop back after you push it, the lid has sealed correctly. If it does pop back up, it hasn't sealed properly, but you can still use the jam—just refrigerate it immediately and use within 2 weeks.

CHERRY–STAR ANISE JAM

So before you judge or say this is a weird combination, hear me out. I am not a fan of anise flavor. I hate that black licorice thing it has happening. *But*, when paired correctly and subtly, it is delicious. It has the power to stand up to the strong tart flavor of cherries and add a nice depth and fun flavor kick.

1 pound fresh or frozen pitted cherries

½ cup sugar

2 small star anise pods

1 In a medium saucepan, combine all the ingredients over medium to high heat. Cook for 15 minutes, then reduce the heat to maintain a simmer. Mash up the cherries with a fork or potato masher and simmer, stirring occasionally, for 20 minutes or more (the cooking time will vary depending on the moisture content of the cherries), until the jam thickens and starts to get shiny and iridescent. Be careful not to overcook the jam, as it can thicken and dry out too much (see Note, page 127).

2 Let the jam cool slightly, then transfer it to clean mason jars or any airtight container you prefer. It will keep in the fridge for up to 2 weeks. For longer storage, follow the canning instructions on page 127.

APPLE BUTTER

Pair this yummy apple butter with warm bread. Or just eat it
with a spoon.

4 pounds Fuji or other preferred
apples, peeled, cored,
and sliced

1 cup granulated sugar

1 cup packed brown sugar

2 teaspoons ground cinnamon

½ teaspoon ground cloves

1 tablespoon vanilla extract

1 tablespoon fresh lemon juice

½ teaspoon fine sea salt

1   Place the apples in a slow cooker.

2   In a small bowl, stir together the granulated sugar, brown sugar,
cinnamon, cloves, vanilla, lemon juice, and salt. Add this mixture to
the apples and stir to coat the apples.

3   Cover the slow cooker and cook on high for 1 hour, then turn the
heat to low and cook for 10 hours, mashing up the apples with a
potato masher halfway through the cooking time.

4   Transfer the apple butter to a blender (or use an immersion blender
directly in the slow cooker) and blend to your desired consistency—
super smooth or kinda chunky.

5   Transfer the apple butter to an airtight container and store in the
refrigerator for up to 2 weeks.

CINNAMON PECAN OATMEAL SCONES

This somewhat healthier version of a scone is not too heavy, and it's reminiscent of morning buns! What's not to love? I've swapped out the typical sour cream and heavy cream for regular milk, and the oatmeal adds a more wholesome element. I served these at my very first restaurant in Costa Rica, and they were a big hit.

SCONES

2 cups all-purpose flour

1 cup old-fashioned or quick-cooking oats

¾ cup granulated sugar

1 tablespoon baking powder

2 teaspoons ground cinnamon

¼ teaspoon fine sea salt

¾ cup chopped pecans

½ cup (1 stick) unsalted butter, cubed and chilled

1 large egg

¾ cup whole milk

1 teaspoon vanilla extract

ICING

1 cup confectioners' sugar, sifted

¼ teaspoon ground cinnamon

1½ tablespoons water

1 **To make the scones:** Preheat the oven to 400°F. Line a baking sheet with parchment paper or a silicone baking mat.

2 In a large bowl, combine the flour, oats, granulated sugar, baking powder, cinnamon, salt, and pecans. Add the butter and, using your fingers, mix until it is broken down into pea-size pieces. Add the egg, milk, and vanilla and stir to combine.

3 Turn the dough out onto a floured surface and roll it into a rectangle. If the dough is super sticky, dust it with flour and gently fold it over itself to mix it in. Cut the dough into roughly 2 by 3- to 4-inch rectangles and place them on the prepared baking sheet. These will double in size, so leave plenty of room between them.

4 Bake until lightly golden brown, about 20 minutes. Let the scones cool.

5 **To make the icing:** In a small bowl, stir together the confectioners' sugar, cinnamon, and water. Drizzle the icing all over the cooled scones.

CRANBERRY-PISTACHIO SCONES

The tartness of cranberries with the sweet nuttiness of pistachios is the perfect scone pairing. And it is delicious any time of year, but especially festive for the holidays as you have your red and green Christmas colors.

2 cups all-purpose flour

⅓ cup sugar, plus more for sprinkling

1 teaspoon baking powder

¼ teaspoon baking soda

½ teaspoon fine sea salt

1 teaspoon orange zest

½ cup dried cranberries, unsweetened

½ cup coarsely chopped pistachios, toasted

½ cup (1 stick) unsalted butter, cubed and chilled

2 large eggs, slightly beaten

¾ cup sour cream

1 teaspoon vanilla extract

¼ cup heavy cream

1   Preheat the oven to 375°F. Line a baking sheet with parchment paper or a silicone baking mat.

2   In a large bowl, whisk together the flour, sugar, baking powder, baking soda, salt, orange zest, cranberries, and pistachios. Add the butter and, using your fingers, mix until it is broken down into pea-size pieces.

3   In a small bowl, stir together the eggs, sour cream, and vanilla. Add the mixture to the dry ingredients and stir to combine.

4   Turn the dough out onto a generously floured surface. (You'll need a lot of flour to keep the dough from sticking and to make it less sticky itself.) Fold the dough over on itself three times and roll it out into a long log, about 18 inches long. Flatten the log to about 3 inches thick. Cut into 2-inch triangles. Place the triangles on the prepared baking sheet, cover, and refrigerate for 30 minutes.

5   Brush the scones with the heavy cream and sprinkle generously with sugar. Bake for 20 to 25 minutes, until the scones are just turning golden brown around the edges and spring back in the center when touched.

BREAKFAST COOKIE

This cookie is my everything. First, because, well, it's a cookie. Second, because it's hearty and filled with lots of dried fruits and nuts, so it's like a little meal on the go. If you haven't noticed already, I love grab-and-go things I can eat on the run with a cup of coffee.

¼ cup packed chopped dried apples

¼ cup chopped dried pineapple

2 tablespoons dried cranberries, unsweetened

3 tablespoons dried blueberries

¼ cup chopped walnuts

1 cup old-fashioned or quick-cooking oats

½ cup all-purpose flour

½ teaspoon baking soda

½ teaspoon fine sea salt

6 tablespoons (¾ stick) unsalted butter

⅓ cup packed dark brown sugar

1 tablespoon honey

1 large egg

1 Preheat the oven to 350°F. Line a baking sheet with parchment paper or a silicone baking mat.

2 In a small bowl, combine the dried apples, pineapple, cranberries, blueberries, and walnuts and set aside.

3 In a separate small bowl, stir together the oats, flour, baking soda, and salt. Set aside.

4 In the bowl of a stand mixer fitted with the whisk, cream the butter until fluffy, then add the brown sugar and honey and beat for a minute or so, until fluffy. Add the egg and mix until combined, stopping and scraping down the sides of the bowl once or twice.

5 Add the oat mixture to the bowl and mix briefly just until the dough starts to come together. Add the dried fruit mixture and mix briefly to combine.

6 Drop large spoonfuls of the dough onto the prepared baking sheet, spacing them a couple inches apart.

7 Bake for about 15 minutes, until lightly golden brown on top with darker edges and deep golden brown on the bottom. Be careful, as these can overbake quickly and get too dark on the bottom. If the top still looks a tiny bit shiny in the middle, that's okay—they will continue to cook after you remove them from the oven. Let cool on the pan and store in an airtight container at room temperature for up to a few days.

BISCUITS, MUFFINS, BREADS & MORE BAKED GOODIES

133

NOTE To supreme the grapefruit before cutting it into pieces, trim the bottom and top off of the grapefruit. Set one of the flat sides on a cutting board and, following the contour of the grapefruit with a knife, slice the peel off of the grapefruit. Hold the peeled grapefruit in your hand over a bowl to catch the juices. Carefully, with a sharp knife, slice in between the membrane and the grapefruit flesh to remove each segment. Once you have removed the segments, you can squeeze excess juice into the bowl to use for the glaze, then cut the segments into smaller pieces.

GRAPEFRUIT-PISTACHIO CAKES

These, to me, are the perfect brunch cakes. They are pretty on the outside and fresh and vibrant on the inside—a nice complement to any brunch feast or even perfect to eat on their own with coffee in the morning.

CAKES

Nonstick cooking spray

1 cup all-purpose flour

½ cup granulated sugar

¼ teaspoon baking soda

¼ teaspoon fine sea salt

½ cup vegetable oil or canola oil

¼ cup buttermilk

1 large egg

¼ teaspoon distilled white vinegar

¼ teaspoon vanilla extract

½ cup chopped fresh grapefruit (¼ to ½-inch pieces; see Note opposite)

¼ cup finely chopped very lightly toasted pistachios, plus more for sprinkling

GLAZE

2 cups confectioners' sugar

Juice of ½ grapefruit, or more if needed (see Note opposite)

NOTE   You can use any mold shape you like for the mini Bundt pan. Or you can use a muffin pan or even bake it as a loaf. For a loaf, your baking time will mostly likely double. Just be sure to watch the browning and cover it with foil if it is darkening too much during baking.

1   **To make the cakes:** Preheat the oven to 350°F. Spray a mini Bundt cake pan (see Note below) with cooking spray.

2   In a medium bowl, whisk together the flour, granulated sugar, baking soda, and salt to combine and aerate.

3   In a separate medium bowl, stir together the oil, buttermilk, egg, vinegar, and vanilla. Add to the dry ingredients and stir to combine. Stir in the grapefruit and pistachios.

4   Fill the prepared molds three-quarters full and bake for 25 to 30 minutes, or until the cake gently springs back when lightly touched. Let the cakes cool in the pan for 10 to 15 minutes.

5   Set a sheet of parchment paper or a baking sheet on the counter, line it with a wire rack, and turn the cakes out onto the rack.

6   **To make the glaze:** In a small bowl, stir together the confectioners' sugar and grapefruit juice. For a thicker glaze, use less juice, or add more for a thinner glaze.

7   Spoon the glaze over the cakes. It's okay to glaze the cakes when they're still warm, as this tends to let the glaze soak in more—yum! You can add as much or little glaze as you like. Immediately after glazing each cake, sprinkle pistachios on top. Be sure to do this quickly before the glaze dries so the pistachios stick.

Almond Croissants, *page 152*

Chocolate Croissants, *page 152*

FANCY PASTRIES

BRIOCHE BEIGNETS

This recipe has been a work in progress for years, starting when I was the executive pastry chef of The Penthouse restaurant of the Huntley Hotel, overlooking the beach in Santa Monica. I loved the recipe so much that later, when I was the pastry chef at the Michelin-starred restaurant Patina, I gave it a fancy facelift and filled the beignets with chocolate ganache and served them on top of a mint chocolate cookie crumble with dehydrated eggless peppermint meringues and eucalyptus ice cream. These are so good—dressed up or dressed down—they are sure to be a favorite. They're simply perfect on their own with coffee. A little fried dough for breakfast is always a good idea. Your only trouble will be deciding whether to sprinkle with cinnamon sugar or confectioners' sugar!

¾ cup all-purpose flour

2 tablespoons granulated sugar

½ teaspoon fine sea salt

1½ teaspoons active dry yeast

1 tablespoon warm water

1 large egg, chilled

5 tablespoons unsalted butter, cubed and chilled

Vegetable oil or canola oil, for frying

Cinnamon sugar (see Note) or confectioners' sugar, for dusting

NOTE   To make cinnamon sugar, combine ¼ cup granulated sugar and 1 teaspoon ground cinnamon.

1   In the bowl of a stand mixer fitted with the paddle attachment, stir together flour, sugar, and salt by hand to combine.

2   In a small bowl, dissolve the yeast with warm water and mix to make a thick paste. Add the paste to the dry flour mixture and mix on low to medium speed until somewhat combined. The mixture will be dry and lumpy.

3   Add the egg and mix on medium speed to combine. If the mixture is very dry and not coming together, add some tepid water 1 teaspoon at a time. Be sure to add it slowly and allow time for it to mix in. You do not want to add too much! The mixture should be just wet enough to come together. Mix on medium to high speed until the mixture starts to stick to itself. This may take up to 5 minutes. Don't worry about overmixing. The key to making bread is allowing time to build up the gluten and protein structure. Yes, that bad word—*gluten* (see sidebar, page 141)!

recipe continues

4 Remove the butter from the fridge. With the mixer on low to medium speed, slowly start adding the butter cube by cube—do not add it too fast or all at once. When all the butter has been added, mix for a few minutes until the dough again begins to combine with itself. It will be very sticky and will not come together completely to form a ball like most doughs. If the mixture appears too shiny and wet-looking, add a little extra flour, 1 teaspoon at a time. You want the dough to be sticky, but not too wet and shiny.

5 Lightly coat a small bowl with oil. Form the dough into a ball and place the dough in the bowl. Place plastic wrap directly on top of the dough and refrigerate for at least 1 hour or up to 24 hours.

6 Fill a medium pot with oil to a depth of about 2 inches and attach a thermometer to the side. Heat the oil over medium to high heat to 350 to 365°F. (If you don't have a thermometer, a good way to test the oil is to dip a piece of dough into it. If the oil bubbles upon contact, it's ready.) When the oil comes to temperature, reduce the heat slightly while you roll out the dough. Have a plate lined with paper towels or a wire rack ready to drain the beignets after frying.

7 Remove the dough from the refrigerator and turn it out onto a floured work surface. Cut it in half and generously sprinkle the top of each half with flour.

8 Roll out one of the halves, making sure to continue adding flour underneath so it doesn't stick to your work surface. (This dough is particularly sticky, so don't be shy with the added flour.) Roll the dough to ⅛-inch thickness, then cut it into 2-inch squares or use a 2-inch cookie or biscuit cutter to cut it into rounds and place them on a plate or baking sheet. Repeat with the second half of the dough. Scraps can be used to make more beignets.

9 Gently drop a few cutouts at a time into the hot oil. Once the bottom sides are a dark golden brown, flip the beignets over to fry the other side. Once the beignets are dark golden brown all over, use a slotted spoon to remove them from the oil and place them on the paper towel–lined plate or rack. If coating with cinnamon sugar, roll the beignets in a bowl of cinnamon sugar immediately after frying so the sugar will stick. If using confectioners' sugar, you can wait until all the batches are done to sprinkle with confectioners' sugar. Repeat to fry the remaining beignets.

FUN FILLINGS

Fill the beignets with cheese, jam, or chocolate to get extra fancy and impress your friends or to add some variety for a fun savory option. My favorite cheese for filling is raclette (it melts perfectly) or Gruyère, though even just some classic Cheddar is great, too; sprinkle with plain salt instead of confectioners' sugar. For chocolate, you can use chocolate chips as the filling. Milk chocolate works well, as it doesn't burn as easily as dark chocolate can. You can also make a flavored ganache to use as a filling. The possibilities are endless. Have fun, experiment, make mistakes, enjoy!

To fill the beignets: Place about a teaspoon of your preferred filling directly into the middle of one of the 2-inch cutouts. Wet your finger with water and gently run your finger around the outer edge of the dough. Place another cutout on top and gently press all around the edges to seal. Repeat with the remaining cutouts. Let sit for a couple of minutes before frying to make sure the edges have sealed—you don't want all the filling leaking out into your fryer oil. (If this does happen, strain the oil through a fine-mesh strainer into a new pot.) You can assemble them ahead of time and store them, covered, in the fridge until ready to fry them; in fact, this is ideal, as it allows the dough to seal and harden up. Pull out from the fridge and fry them when you're ready.

GOOD GLUTEN?

Although sometimes thought of as a "bad word," gluten is a naturally occurring protein crucial to making bread dough and similar doughs. Gluten is activated when water is added to flour. As you mix and knead the dough, the proteins develop, creating a structure that lends strength and elasticity to the dough. This structure expands and holds the gases that are released during baking, giving bread its rise . . . and allowing beignets to pop up into fluffy pillows without bursting! Gluten is what makes those pockets of air you see when you slice into bread, and it's what gives bread its not-too-dense texture. Thank you, gluten! Bread just isn't the same without you!

FRIED DOUGHNUTS

Yes, yes, I know what you are thinking: *a fried doughnut?!?!* Yes, a fried doughnut. There's nothing wrong with the original creation that inspired my *baked* doughnut bakery. In fact, if you are talking about this recipe, I should open up a fried doughnut shop. They are crispy, light, and fluffy. Top them with different glazes, sprinkles, or freeze-dried fruit, or fill them with custard. Have fun—isn't that what doughnuts are all about?

DOUGHNUTS

2 cups all-purpose flour

2½ tablespoons granulated sugar

½ teaspoon fine sea salt

¾ cup warm milk

1⅛ teaspoons active dry yeast

1 large egg

4 tablespoons (½ stick) unsalted butter, cubed and chilled

Vegetable oil or canola oil, for frying

VANILLA GLAZE

1 cup confectioners' sugar, plus more if needed

1 teaspoon vanilla extract

1½ to 2 tablespoons water

— *and/or* —

CHOCOLATE GLAZE

1 cup confectioners' sugar, plus more if needed

1 tablespoon unsweetened dark cocoa powder

2 tablespoons water

1 **To make the doughnuts:** In the bowl of a stand mixer fitted with the dough hook, stir together the flour, sugar, and salt by hand.

2 Put the warm milk in a small bowl or measuring cup and add the yeast. Stir to dissolve the yeast, then add it to the flour mixture. Mix on medium-low speed. Add the egg. Mix until combined and the dough becomes elastic and shiny.

3 Add the butter and mix until the dough is smooth, shiny, and stretchy.

4 Turn out the dough onto a floured surface. Fold the dough over on itself a few times and then roll it into a ball and place it in a lightly buttered bowl. Cover the bowl and and set aside for 1 hour, until doubled in size.

5 Turn the dough out onto a floured surface and roll it to about ¼ inch thick. Using a doughnut cutter or large round cookie cutter, cut out circles from the dough. If using a cookie cutter, use a small circle to cut out the centers. (You can save the centers for doughnut holes.) Bring the dough scraps together into a rough ball and set aside. Place the cutout doughnuts on a sheet of parchment paper or a baking sheet and loosely cover them with plastic wrap.

recipe continues

TOPPINGS, GLAZES, AND FILLINGS

My favorite **doughnut toppings** are freeze-dried fruit, such as strawberries, blueberries, mango, and pineapple. I like to break the fruit into pieces and sprinkle it on top of the doughnut just after glazing. Be sure to do this to each doughnut *immediately* after glazing when the glaze is still wet so the fruit will stick. (This applies for sprinkles, too.)

To get creative with the glaze, follow the recipe for vanilla glaze but use any juice (for example, grapefruit, lemon, lime, or blueberry juice) to replace the water. You could also blend fresh strawberries to make a strawberry glaze by using the blended strawberries in place of juice. The possibilities for fun, flavored doughnut glazes are endless. And just like you can pair a vanilla glaze with freeze-dried strawberries, you could also do a lime glaze with freeze-dried pineapple. Mix and match to your palate's delight.

Try fillings, too! Use custard or jam to fill doughnuts—try the recipes for banana custard (page 82), vanilla custard (page 84), or jam (pages 125 and 128): Fit a pastry bag with a very small piping tip and fill it with the custard or jam (or use a small resealable plastic bag with one corner snipped off). Make three different holes equally spaced out around the side of a cooked doughnut and gently squeeze the custard or jam into the doughnut.

6 Roll out the remaining dough and cut out more doughnuts until you have no usable dough left (it's okay to discard that last bit of dough, as it's been handled a lot and will not give you as light of a doughnut).

7 Let the doughnuts proof for 20 to 40 minutes, depending on the temperature and environment where the doughnuts proof. The best indicator is the finger test: if you press the dough and it gently rises back but an indentation remains, it has proofed enough and you are ready to fry. (For more on proofing, see page 148).

8 *To make the vanilla glaze or chocolate glaze:* Combine all the glaze ingredients with the water and whisk until smooth and free of lumps. You want a syrupy, honey-like consistency—thick but runny. Add more water or sugar to get the desired consistency.

NOTE Keep the thermometer in the oil, as the temperature will change when you add the doughnuts and as the frying goes on. You may need to adjust the heat under the oil as you go to keep the oil between 350 and 365°F.

9 Fill a large pot with oil to a depth of 2 to 3 inches and attach a thermometer to the side. Heat the oil over medium to high heat to 360°F (see Note). Line your counter with some paper towels and set a wire rack on top.

10 Gently place 2 to 4 doughnuts in the oil, depending on the size of the pot—do not overcrowd the pot. Fry for 2 to 3 minutes on each side, until nicely golden brown. Once done, use a slotted spoon or strainer to remove them from the oil, letting excess oil drip off (you can gently shake them to help this, but be careful of the hot oil), and place them on the rack to drain.

11 Let the doughnuts cool slightly, pour over the glaze, let the glaze set for a few minutes, and enjoy!

CINNAMON ROLLS

DOUGH

3½ cups all-purpose flour

¼ cup granulated sugar

1¼ teaspoons fine sea salt

1 cup warm whole milk

2¼ teaspoons active dry yeast

1 large egg

1 teaspoon vanilla extract

5 tablespoons unsalted butter

FILLING

½ cup (1 stick) unsalted butter, softened at room temperature

1 cup packed dark brown sugar

2 tablespoons ground cinnamon

½ teaspoon fine sea salt

FROSTING

½ cup confectioners' sugar, sifted

½ (8-ounce) package cream cheese, at room temperature

2 tablespoons unsalted butter, at room temperature

1 teaspoon vanilla extract

2 teaspoons whole milk

¼ teaspoon fine sea salt

TOPPING

1 tablespoon unsalted butter

¼ cup heavy cream

Cinnamon rolls remind me of my childhood. Though let me clarify: we used the Pillsbury ones you pop out of the tube, which I always loved but which terrified me in equal measure. That thing really pops! As a child, I always fought and demanded to be able to smear the frosting all over the tops after they were finished baking. The cinnamon smell, the warm, ooey-gooey frosting-covered dough— there is nothing like it. This is more work than the store-bought stuff, but homemade from scratch is always so much better and so much more rewarding after all that work. You can eat that cinnamon roll guilt-free—you earned it!

1 **To make the dough:** In the bowl of a stand mixer fitted with the dough hook, stir together the flour, granulated sugar, and salt by hand.

2 Put the warm milk in a small bowl or measuring cup and add the yeast. Stir to dissolve the yeast, then add it to the flour mixture. Add the egg and vanilla. Mix on low to medium speed for 2 minutes, until the dough comes together in a ball and sticks to itself, but is still a little wet and sticky. If the dough doesn't come together within the first 2 minutes of mixing, add more milk, 1 tablespoon at a time, and mix after each addition to see if it comes together. Alternatively, if the dough is overly wet or sticky, slowly add 1 tablespoon flour at a time. Mix on medium speed for another 5 minutes, or until the dough has good elasticity.

3 Slowly add the butter and mix for 5 minutes more, or until the dough comes together again in a smooth ball. Once the dough is stretchy and does not break apart easily when pulled, turn it out onto a floured surface. Fold the dough over on itself a few times and shape it into a ball. Place the dough in a lightly floured or oiled bowl. Loosely cover

recipe continues

THE PROOF, THE WHOLE PROOF, AND NOTHING BUT THE PROOF

Okay. So proofing dough is a tricky art. Most home recipes will just say to let the dough double in size. In my opinion, this leaves a lot of room for error or overproofing. One thing that happens when you allow your dough to overproof is that it will taste yeasty, sour, or tart. This is not a yummy thing. On the other side, if you underproof, the dough will not have the rise and correct airy texture. So how the heck do you know when it's done? I'm here to tell you. Like testing cakes to see if they are done baking, it's all in your pointer finger. When your dough is perfectly proofed, it will slowly spring back after being gently poked but still have an indentation from your finger. I recommend you start poking after 20 minutes, and if it's not ready, check every 5 to 10 minutes after that. If your kitchen is on the cooler side and you can tell by looking at the dough that it has not risen at all, you can wait a bit longer before you start checking. There should be some rise in the dough but it will not quite double—think more like 25 percent larger. Another important thing to note is to gently cover the dough or to spritz it with water. You don't want the dough to form a "crust" while proofing—you want it moist so it can stretch freely.

with plastic wrap. Set aside at room temperature (or slightly warmer) to rise for 1 to 1½ hours, until almost doubled in size.

4   **To make the filling:** While the dough is rising, in a small bowl, combine the butter, brown sugar, cinnamon, and salt. Mix until fully combined.

5   Lightly grease a large baking dish.

6   Turn the dough out onto a floured surface. Flatten the dough and roll it out in a rectangle ⅛ to ¼ inch thick (it doesn't have to be a perfect rectangle, just as close as you can get to a rectangular shape). Spread the filling over the dough, covering the entire surface. With one long side of the dough facing you, gently roll it up into a log, being careful not to roll it too tightly or too loosely. Slice the log crosswise into pieces ¾ to 1 inch thick. (I usually discard the first two pieces on each end because they are generally uneven, but you can save them and use them if you like.)

7   Place the rolls in the prepared baking dish, cut-side up, leaving at least ½ inch between them, as they rise during proofing and grow more during baking. (Depending on the size of your baking dish, you may need a second dish.) Gently cover the cinnamon rolls with plastic wrap and set aside in a warm place for 30 to 40 minutes to proof and puff up. (For more on proofing, see left.)

8   Preheat the oven to 350°F.

9   **To make the frosting:** While the cinnamon rolls are proofing, in a medium bowl, combine all the frosting ingredients. Use a handheld mixer or stir by hand until smooth.

10 **To make the topping:** Once the cinnamon rolls have proofed, in a small pot, combine the butter and heavy cream and heat over medium-low heat until the butter has melted. Brush the tops of the cinnamon rolls with this mixture.

11 Bake for 30 to 40 minutes, until the cinnamon rolls are light golden brown.

12 Remove from the oven and let cool for a couple of minutes. While they are still warm, spread the frosting all over the top and enjoy.

CROISSANTS

Croissants are amazing. This is the ultimate recipe to make you feel like a real pro in the kitchen and impress your friends—not to mention the benefit of getting to eat truly freshly baked croissants. Don't be intimidated by this recipe. Try, try, and try again, if at first you don't succeed. What's the worst that can happen? You try to be a badass in the kitchen and make homemade croissants and they don't turn out? That's more than most can say.

3¼ cups all-purpose flour, plus more if needed

6 tablespoons sugar

2 tablespoons dry milk powder

2 tablespoons fine sea salt

1 tablespoon active dry yeast

1¼ cups plus 2 tablespoons warm water

½ teaspoon vanilla extract

1 large egg, plus 1 beaten egg for egg wash

1½ cups plus 2 tablespoons (3¼ sticks) unsalted butter, at room temperature

1 In the bowl of a stand mixer fitted with the dough hook, combine the flour, sugar, dry milk powder, and salt. Mix to combine.

2 Place the yeast in a bowl (I prefer to use a glass bowl so I can make sure there is no undissolved yeast at the bottom of the bowl after whisking) and add the warm water. Let sit for 30 seconds, then whisk to dissolve the yeast.

3 With the mixer running on low, slowly pour in the yeast mixture. Add the vanilla. Increase the mixer speed to medium-high and mix until the dough comes together in a ball, then add the egg and 2 tablespoons of the butter. Mix until the egg and butter are incorporated, stopping and scraping down the sides and bottom of the bowl as needed.

4 Mix until the dough forms a ball again and makes a slapping sound against the mixer bowl. The bowl should be clean and all the dough should be smooth, elastic, and self-contained in a nice smooth ball. If, after a couple of minutes of mixing, the dough seems very wet and sticky and is not coming together, slowly add more flour 1 to 2 tablespoons at a time. Work slowly—you don't want to add too much flour—and mix on medium-high for at least a minute before adding more flour. (Dough making is easily affected by temperature

recipe continues

and humidity, so each time you make it, the amount of flour you need can be different—I have had to add almost as much as an additional ½ cup flour to my dough on occasion.)

5   Turn the dough out onto a lightly floured surface. Fold the dough over on itself and shape it into a firm ball. Place the dough in a lightly floured or oiled bowl. Gently dust the top of the dough with flour and loosely cover with plastic wrap. Set aside on the counter for 1 hour.

6   While the dough is resting, take a large sheet of plastic wrap, squish the remaining 1½ cups (3 sticks) butter on top of the plastic, and place another sheet of plastic on top. Roll out the softened butter into a roughly 10-inch square. Refrigerate the butter while the dough rests.

7   Roll the rested dough into a rectangle roughly 12 by 18 inches—again, not looking for perfection, just as close as you can. Remove the butter from the fridge. While it is still covered in plastic, gently beat the butter with a rolling pin to soften it and make it malleable and easier to work with. You need the butter to be soft enough to roll out and work with, but still cold.

8   Remove both pieces of plastic and place the butter in the center of the rolled-out dough. Wrap the edges of the dough over the butter to completely cover it, then fold the ends of the dough so they meet the center and then fold in half.

9   Use your finger to make an indentation in the dough. (This is letting you know you have folded the dough once.) Wrap the dough in plastic and refrigerate for at least 30 minutes—1 hour is best.

10   Remove the dough, roll it out into a long rectangle. Fold the ends in toward the center to meet and then fold in half. Don't panic if at this point your butter layer is breaking into smaller pieces you can see underneath the dough as you roll it out. It won't affect the end result. Use your finger to make two indentations in the dough to indicate you've completed the second fold.

11   Repeat the process until you have folded the dough four times. (Trust me, the finger marks help. I always forget after the first few times how many times I have folded it. More folds is better, as it creates more layers, but you can end up overworking the dough.) Refrigerate the dough for at least 1 hour and up to 12 hours. Don't worry if you can't complete all of the folding in one day. Just don't let the dough sit in the refrigerator for more than 24 hours. I usually start the dough one day and finish the next.

12   Line a baking sheet with parchment paper or a silicone baking mat.

13   On a floured surface, roll the dough out into a ¼-inch-thick rectangle. Trim the dough into a long strip about 6 inches wide. Cut the strip into triangles about 3 inches wide at the bottom and 6 inches long.

14   Roll each triangle so it is thinner, stretching it longer. Working with one triangle at a time, with the wide part closest to you, pull the corners out to the sides to stretch the dough, then gently roll the triangle up from the wide end to the point. Place the rolled triangles on the prepared baking sheet with the points on the bottom.

recipe continues

15 If you have the time to spritz the proofing croissants with water every 20 minutes, you do not need to cover them in plastic wrap. If you will not be able to spritz them every 20 minutes, spritz them once, then gently cover them with plastic wrap. Set them aside in a warm spot (see Note) to proof until increased in size by 25 percent. This can take anywhere from 30 minutes to over an hour, depending on the temperature and environment where the croissants rest. The best indicator is the finger test: if you press the dough and it gently rises back but an indentation remains, it has proofed enough and you are ready to bake. (For more on proofing, see page 148.)

16 Preheat the oven to 425°F on convection bake if your oven has a convection setting. If your oven does not have a convection setting, preheat it to 450°F.

17 Brush the croissants with the egg wash. Place the baking sheet in the oven and immediately reduce the oven temperature to 375°F (if using convection) or 400°F (if using a conventional oven). Spray some water inside the oven, close the door, and bake for about 10 minutes, until very deep golden brown, rotating the baking sheet halfway through the cooking time. If baking on convection, keep a close eye on the croissants—they can brown very quickly and almost burn. Let croissants cool slightly before eating. Keep in an airtight container or loosely wrap in foil. Keep at room temperature. Can be stored for up to 3 days.

NOTE A warm place in your kitchen is fine for proofing, but I like to take it one step further. Please don't feel like you have to take that step with me—I'm passing it along in case you'd like to try it. I usually proof my croissants in a small closet or bathroom. I place a small space heater on low in the same room, at least 3 or 4 feet away from the croissants, and spritz them with water every 20 minutes (or spritz them once, then gently cover with plastic wrap if I don't have time to do it every 20 minutes).

PROSCIUTTO-GRUYÈRE CROISSANTS When you have rolled out and stretched the triangles of dough, lay a slice of prosciutto on top of each and sprinkle with about 1 tablespoon shredded Gruyère cheese before gently rolling them up.

CHOCOLATE CROISSANTS Cut the dough into 2 by 4-inch rectangles instead of triangles. Place approximately 1 tablespoon dark chocolate pieces on the bottom third of the dough, then fold the bottom up over the chocolate and fold that over. Place the croissants seam-side down on the baking sheet.

ALMOND CROISSANTS Make the frangipane filling from the Almond Frangipane and Pear Baked French Toast (page 91). Once you've rolled and stretched the triangles, spread the almond frangipane filling over the dough and gently roll them up. Be careful not to spread the filling too close to the edges and not to roll too tightly. Brush the croissants with the egg wash and sprinkle with sliced almonds. Bake as directed, then dust with confectioners' sugar after baking.

step 13

step 13

step 13

step 14

STICKY BUNS

Sticky bun vs. cinnamon roll. What's your preference? If I had to pick, I'd have to say I'm a cinnamon roll gal, but . . . sometimes you just need that sticky, chewiness of a sticky bun with the good crunchy texture of raisins and nuts! Good thing for you, you can have both and you can even make one batch of dough and split it and make half cinnamon rolls and half sticky buns. You read me right! Make everybody in the family happy. I like options.

DOUGH

3½ cups all-purpose flour

¼ cup granulated sugar

1¼ teaspoons fine sea salt

1 cup warm whole milk

2¼ teaspoons active dry yeast

1 large egg

1 teaspoon vanilla extract

6 tablespoons (¾ stick) unsalted butter

¼ cup heavy cream

FILLING

¾ cup (1½ sticks) unsalted butter, at room temperature

1½ cups granulated sugar

2 tablespoons ground cinnamon

Pinch of fine sea salt

½ cup raisins

BASE

1 cup (2 sticks) unsalted butter, at room temperature

1 cup packed brown sugar

¼ cup honey

1 teaspoon vanilla extract

1¼ cups chopped pecans

1 tablespoon bourbon

Pinch of fine sea salt

TOPPING

1 tablespoon unsalted butter

¼ cup heavy cream

1 *To make the dough:* In the bowl of a stand mixer fitted with the hook attachment, stir together the flour, granulated sugar, and salt by hand.

2 Put the warm milk in a small bowl or measuring cup and add the yeast. Stir to dissolve the yeast, then add it to the flour mixture. Add the egg and vanilla. Mix on low to medium speed for 2 minutes, until the dough comes together in a ball and sticks to itself, but is still a little wet and sticky. If the dough doesn't come together within the first 2 minutes of mixing, add more milk, 1 tablespoon at a time, and mix after each addition to see if it comes together. Alternatively, if the dough is overly wet or sticky, slowly add 1 tablespoon flour at a time.

Mix on medium speed for another 5 minutes, or until the dough has good elasticity.

3 Slowly add 5 tablespoons of the butter and continue mixing for 5 minutes more, until the dough comes together again in a smooth ball. Once the dough is stretchy and does not break apart easily when pulled, turn it out onto a floured surface. Fold the dough over on itself a few times and shape it into a ball. Place the dough in a lightly floured or oiled bowl. Loosely cover it with plastic wrap. Let it rise at room temperature (or slightly warmer) for 1 to 1½ hours until almost doubled in size.

4 *To make the filling:* While the dough is rising, in the bowl of a stand mixer fitted with the paddle attachment, cream the butter. Add the granulated sugar, cinnamon, and pinch of salt. Mix until fully combined. Stir in the raisins by hand.

5 Turn the dough out onto a floured surface. Flatten the dough and roll it out to a rectangle, or as close to a rectangle as you can, roughly ⅛ to ¼ inch thick. Spread the filling over the dough, covering the entire surface. (If the filling is too stiff to spread, microwave it for 20 seconds or so to soften it.)

6 With one long side of the dough facing you, gently roll up the dough into a log, being careful not to roll it too tightly or too loosely. Slice the log crosswise into pieces ¾ to 1 inch thick. (I usually discard the first two pieces on each end because they are generally uneven, but you can save them and use them if you like.)

7 *To make the base:* In the bowl of a stand mixer fitted with the paddle attachment, cream the butter. Add the brown sugar, honey, vanilla, pecans, bourbon, and salt. Mix until combined. Spread the mixture evenly over the bottom of a 9 by 11-inch (or similar size) baking dish.

8 Place the buns in the baking dish over the base, cut-side down, leaving ½ to 1 inch between them, as they will rise during proofing and grow more during baking. Gently cover the buns with plastic wrap and set aside in a warm place for 30 to 40 minutes to proof and puff up. (For more on proofing, see page 148.)

9 *To make the topping:* Once the sticky buns have proofed, in a small pot, combine the butter and heavy cream and heat over medium-low heat until the butter has melted. Brush the tops of the sticky buns with this mixture.

10 Preheat the oven to 350°F.

11 Bake the buns for 35 to 45 minutes, until they're nice and golden brown. Remove them from the oven and immediately carefully flip them out of the dish onto a sheet of foil or a silicone baking mat. (You must do this immediately because if you let the base cool, it will harden and stick and you won't be able to remove the buns from the baking dish.) The ooey-gooey base layer now becomes the sticky, gooey top layer of your delicious buns.

PREP TIME: 20 minutes   TOTAL TIME: 1 hour 45 minutes   YIELD: Makes one 10-inch tart, to serve 8

APPLE-ALMOND TART WITH ORANGE ESSENCE

This tart very well can be served for dessert, but for me it brings to mind the quintessential sophisticated European breakfast pastry. It goes perfectly with coffee and at first bite makes me feel like I'm sitting at a Parisian sidewalk café, sipping espresso and being fancy!

SWEET TART DOUGH (PÂTE SUCRÉE)

1½ cups plus 1 tablespoon all-purpose flour

¾ cup confectioners' sugar, sifted

½ teaspoon fine sea salt

½ cup plus 2 tablespoons (1¼ sticks) unsalted butter, at room temperature

1 large egg

ALMOND FILLING (FRANGIPANE)

3 tablespoons plus 1 teaspoon all-purpose flour

½ cup granulated sugar

1 cup slivered almonds

¼ teaspoon fine sea salt

6 tablespoons (¾ stick) unsalted butter

2 large eggs

1 teaspoon vanilla extract

½ teaspoon orange zest

⅛ teaspoon almond extract (optional)

2 teaspoons bourbon (optional)

TOPPING

2 or 3 apples (Granny Smith for a more tart flavor, Fuji or Golden Delicious for sweet—or use combination)

Juice of ½ orange (reserve the other half for zesting)

Juice of 1 lemon wedge

2 tablespoons unsalted butter, melted

Granulated sugar, for sprinkling

1   **To make the sweet tart dough:** In a food processor, combine the flour, confectioners' sugar, and salt. Pulse a few times just to combine. Add the butter and pulse until almost completely combined. Add the egg and mix until the dough just comes together. Do not overmix. (Alternatively, in the bowl of a stand mixer fitted with the paddle attachment, beat the butter until fluffy. Add the confectioners' sugar and mix until fluffy, scraping down the sides and bottom of the bowl occasionally. Add the egg and mix until almost combined, then add the flour and salt and mix to fully combine. Do not overmix.)

2   Pat the dough into a flat disc. Wrap it in plastic wrap and refrigerate for at least 30 minutes and up to 24 hours. You can also freeze the dough at this point and use it later.

3   Roll the dough out on a lightly floured surface into a round ¼ inch thick. Place it in a 10-inch or

recipe continues

similar size round tart mold, making sure to press it firmly into the inside edges. Neatly trim off any overhanging dough.

4   Refrigerate the tart shell while you make the filling and prepare the apple topping.

5   **To make the almond filling:** In a food processor, combine the flour, granulated sugar, almonds, and salt. Pulse until the almonds are finely ground. Add the butter and pulse until smooth. Add the eggs, vanilla, orange zest, almond extract, and bourbon (if using). Pulse until smooth and combined.

6   Preheat the oven to 375°F.

7   **To make the topping:** Core and segment the apples, then very thinly slice them. Put the slices in a large bowl with the orange juice and lemon juice and toss to combine.

8   Remove the tart shell from the refrigerator and gently prick the bottom all over with a fork. Spread the filling into the tart shell.

9   Arrange the slices over the filling in the tart, starting from the outside in, placing the rounded outer edge of the apple slices on the outside edge of the tart and overlapping each slice and layer of slices, until the tart is completely covered.

10 Brush the tart with the melted butter, then sprinkle with granulated sugar.

11 Bake for about 30 minutes, until golden brown and the frangipane has risen and fluffed up and springs back to the touch, rotating the pan halfway through the baking time.

12 Let the tart cool. Grate fresh orange zest from the reserved orange half over the top before serving.

STRAWBERRY TARTS

This tart will have you forgetting about the breakfast treat you grew up with. Savor the fresh big chunks of fruit and lightly sweetened dough, and if you really want to go all out, top it with some strawberry glaze.

DOUGH

1¼ cups all-purpose flour

2 teaspoons granulated sugar

¼ teaspoon fine sea salt

½ cup (1 stick) unsalted butter, cubed and chilled

1 large egg

Ice water, if needed

FILLING

1½ cups chopped strawberries

⅓ cup granulated sugar

½ teaspoon lemon zest

1 tablespoon all-purpose flour

1 teaspoon vanilla extract

ASSEMBLY

1 egg, beaten, for egg wash

Granulated sugar, for sprinkling (optional)

GLAZE (OPTIONAL)

¼ cup chopped fresh strawberries

1 cup confectioners' sugar

NOTE   Have the dough prepared and ready to go before you make the filling. The longer the filling sits, the juicier it gets, making it more difficult to build the tarts.

1   **To make the dough:** In a food processor, combine the flour, granulated sugar, and salt. Pulse once or twice just to combine. Add the butter and pulse two or three times. Add the egg and pulse until the egg is combined into the dough. If the dough is still dry, add ice water to the dough, 1 tablespoon at a time, just until it becomes moist. The dough may still look crumbly and not be coming together, but if you pinch the dough between your fingers, it should hold together.

2   Turn the dough out onto a lightly floured surface. Fold the dough over on itself once or twice (only fold it over a couple times so you don't overwork the dough). Flatten the dough into a disc or a rectangle about ¼ inch thick. Wrap the dough in plastic wrap and refrigerate for at least 1 hour or up to 24 hours.

3   Roll out the chilled dough to about ⅛ inch thick. Cut into eight 5 by 3-inch rectangles.

4   Preheat the oven to 375°F. Line a baking sheet with parchment paper or a silicone baking mat.

5   **To make the filling:** In a medium bowl, stir together the strawberries, granulated sugar, lemon zest, flour, and vanilla. (See Note.)

recipe continues

6   *To assemble the tarts:* Place ¼ to ⅓ cup of the filling in the center of 4 dough rectangles. Dip your finger in water and wet the edges of the rectangles. If any juice from the filling seeps to the edge of the dough, use a paper towel to soak it up. You want to try to keep the edges as clean as possible so the yummy juices don't leak out during baking.

7   Take one of the unfilled dough rectangles and pull it gently to stretch it a bit, first crosswise, then lengthwise. Place it on top of one of the rectangles with the strawberry filling and press firmly around the edges to seal. Use a fork to crimp the outer ¼ inch of the dough all the way around the edges. With a knife, gently cut a small vent in the top center of the dough. Place the tart on the prepared baking sheet and repeat to assemble 3 more tarts.

8   Brush the tarts with the egg wash. If you are not using the glaze, sprinkle them generously with granulated sugar. Bake for 25 to 30 minutes, until golden brown. Remove from the oven and let cool.

9   *To make the glaze (if using):* Blend the strawberries in a blender until somewhat smooth. Transfer the strawberries to a bowl and stir in the confectioners' sugar. Add water 1 tablespoon at a time, stirring after each, until the glaze reaches your desired consistency. Drizzle the glaze generously on top of the cooled tarts.

BUZZING BLUEBERRY TARTS

Yes, I am adding Earl Grey tea to blueberries again (see page 103). But it really is because it is that good. No, I am not Earl Grey obsessed—I never even drink it as tea. I always like to add additional layers of flavor to my pastries, and the aromatic quality of this tea gives the tarts a certain subtle something. The tea also helps accentuate the blueberry taste, adding more depth to the flavor.

DOUGH

1¼ cups all-purpose flour

2 teaspoons sugar

¼ teaspoon fine sea salt

½ cup (1 stick) unsalted butter, cubed and chilled

1 large egg

Ice water, if needed

FILLING

6 ounces blueberries

⅓ cup sugar

1 tablespoon all-purpose flour

Large pinch of lemon zest

1 teaspoon vanilla extract

1 Earl Grey tea bag

ASSEMBLY

1 egg, beaten, for egg wash

Sugar, for sprinkling

1 **To make the dough:** In a food processor, combine the flour, sugar, and salt. Pulse once or twice just to combine. Add the butter and pulse two or three times. Add the egg and pulse until the egg is combined into the dough. If the dough is still dry, add ice water to the dough, 1 tablespoon at a time, just until it becomes moist. The dough may still look crumbly and not be coming together, but if you pinch the dough between your fingers, it should hold together.

2 Turn the dough out onto a lightly floured surface. Fold the dough over on itself once or twice (only fold it over a couple times so you don't overwork the dough). Flatten the dough into a disc or a rectangle about ¼ inch thick. Wrap the dough in plastic wrap and refrigerate for at least 1 hour or up to 24 hours.

3 Roll out the chilled dough to about ⅛ inch thick. Cut it into eight 5 by 3-inch rectangles.

4 Preheat the oven to 375°F. Line a baking sheet with parchment paper or a silicone baking mat.

NOTE Have the dough prepared and ready to go before you make the filling. Immediately after making the filling, complete the tarts. The longer the filling sits, the juicier it gets, making it more difficult to build the tarts.

5 *To make the filling:* In a medium bowl, combine the blueberries, sugar, flour, lemon zest, and vanilla. Cut open the tea bag and add the tea leaves to the bowl. Stir to combine. With a fork or potato masher, gently mash the blueberries a little bit. (See Note.)

6 *To assemble the tarts:* Place ¼ to ⅓ cup of the filling in the center of 4 dough rectangles. Dip your finger in water and wet the edges of the rectangles. If any juice from the filling seeps to the edge of the dough, use a paper towel to soak it up. You want to try to keep the edges as clean as possible so the yummy juices don't leak out during baking.

7 Take one of the unfilled dough rectangles and pull it gently to stretch it a bit, first crosswise, then lengthwise. Place it on top of one of the rectangles with the blueberry filling and press firmly around the edges to seal. Use a fork to crimp the outer ¼ inch of the dough all the way around the edges. With a knife, gently cut a small vent in the top center of the dough. Place the tart on the prepared baking sheet and repeat to assemble 3 more tarts.

8 Brush the tarts with the egg wash and sprinkle generously with sugar. Bake for 25 to 30 minutes, until golden brown.

RASPBERRY-ORANGE TARTS

This combination of raspberry and orange is bright and tart, the prefect wake-up, grab-and-go treat. The glaze helps balance the tartness of the fresh fruit and makes it a bit more indulgent.

DOUGH

1¼ cups all-purpose flour

2 teaspoons granulated sugar

¼ teaspoon fine sea salt

½ cup (1 stick) unsalted butter, cubed and chilled

1 large egg

Ice water, if needed

FILLING

6 ounces raspberries

⅓ cup plus 2 tablespoons granulated sugar

1 tablespoon all-purpose flour

1 teaspoon orange zest

2 tablespoons chopped orange segments

ASSEMBLY

1 egg, beaten, for egg wash

GLAZE

½ cup confectioners' sugar

¼ teaspoon orange zest

2¼ teaspoons water

1   **To make the dough:** In a food processor, combine the flour, granulated sugar, and salt. Pulse once or twice just to combine. Add the butter and pulse two or three times. Add the egg and pulse until the egg is combined into dough. If the dough is still dry, add ice water to the dough, 1 tablespoon at a time, just until it becomes moist. The dough may still look crumbly and not be coming together, but if you pinch the dough between your fingers, it should hold together.

2   Turn the dough out onto a lightly floured surface. Fold the dough over on itself once or twice (only fold it over a couple times so you don't overwork the dough). Flatten the dough into a disc or a rectangle about ¼ inch thick. Wrap the dough in plastic wrap and refrigerate for at least 1 hour or up to 24 hours.

NOTE Have the dough prepared and ready to go before you make the filling. Immediately after making the filling, complete the tarts. The longer the filling sits, the juicier it gets, making it more difficult to build the tarts.

3 Roll out the chilled dough to about ⅛ inch thick. Cut into eight 5 by 3-inch rectangles.

4 Preheat the oven to 375°F. Line a baking sheet with parchment paper or a silicone baking mat.

5 *To make the filling:* In a medium bowl, stir together the raspberries, granulated sugar, flour, orange zest, and chopped orange. With a fork or potato masher, gently mash the raspberries a little bit. (See Note.)

6 *To assemble the tarts:* Place ¼ to ⅓ cup of the filling in the center of 4 dough rectangles. Dip your finger in water and wet the edges of the rectangles. If any juice from the filling seeps to the edge of the dough, use a paper towel to soak it up. You want to try to keep the edges as clean as possible so the yummy juices don't leak out during baking.

7 Take one of the unfilled dough rectangles and pull it gently to stretch it a bit, first crosswise, then lengthwise. Place it on top of one of the rectangles with the raspberry filling and press firmly around the edges to seal. Use a fork to crimp the outer ¼ inch of the dough all the way around the edges. With a knife, gently cut a small vent in the top center of the dough. Place the tart on the prepared baking sheet and repeat to assemble 3 more tarts.

8 Brush the tarts with the egg wash. Bake for 25 to 30 minutes, until golden brown. Remove from the oven and let cool.

9 *To make the glaze:* In a small bowl, stir together the confectioners' sugar, orange zest, and water. Drizzle the glaze generously on top of the cooled tarts.

YOGURT, BARS, BREAKFAST POPS, SMOOTHIES

& OTHER HEALTHY YUMS

HOMEMADE YOGURT

I love yogurt! It's the perfect snack. It's great in smoothies, in ice pops, with fruit, with granola, on savory dishes—the list goes on and on. I prefer homemade yogurt because it tastes more natural and fresh, and it doesn't have all the added sugar like most store-bought yogurts do. It's also so much creamier and lighter in consistency. Wait, did I mention it is super affordable to make, too? Have fun.

1 quart whole milk

¼ cup plain yogurt with live and active cultures (use a yogurt you prefer, as it will flavor the batch you make; full-fat yogurt is best)

TAKING YOUR TEMPERATURE

Thermometers are a must for every kitchen. There are meat ones, candy ones, frying ones. It can be overwhelming. I like to have one multiuse thermometer. I use a digital one that has a high-temp readout of up to 400°F or close to that. That way, I can use it for everything as it has a high range of temperatures. Digital makes it easy to read, and on most of them you can set an alarm to your desired temp so you know when you have reached it. Also, it has a long cord with a metal thermometer that makes it easy to stick into hot oil or to reach into the oven or the grill to take the temperature of cooked meats.

1 In a small Dutch oven or pot, heat the milk to 190°F. Remove the milk from the heat and let cool to 110 to 115°F. Stir 1 cup of the cooled milk into the yogurt until combined. Add the yogurt mixture to the remaining milk in the pot and gently stir together.

2 Put a lid on the pot and set it aside in a warm place for 5 to 10 hours. (I like to place the pot on a heating pad set to medium heat and cover it with a kitchen towel. I check the temperature frequently, but it's not necessary. If your oven stays warm with the light on, you can place the pot there. You want the temperature to stay between 100°F and 110°F.) After 5 hours, start checking the yogurt for thickness; the longer it sits, the thicker it gets. The time will also depend on the temperature. Once the yogurt reaches your desired thickness, stir it very gently and place it in the fridge to cool and set. Transfer the yogurt to an airtight container and store in the fridge. It will keep for 2 weeks refrigerated. Enjoy!

3 Save some of this batch of yogurt to make your next batch.

YOGURT, BARS, BREAKFAST POPS, SMOOTHIES & OTHER HEALTHY YUMS

169

GRANOLA

2 cups old-fashioned rolled oats

½ cup raw pumpkin seeds

¾ cup sliced almonds

1 cup chopped pecans

3 tablespoons flaxseeds

½ cup shredded coconut (I use sweetened, but you don't have to)

2 tablespoons brown sugar

¼ teaspoon ground cinnamon

½ teaspoon fine sea salt

5 tablespoons honey

¼ cup unsweetened applesauce

2 tablespoons coconut oil, melted

½ teaspoon vanilla extract

½ cup chopped dried apricot

Okay, I *love* granola, but let's be real, most of the time it's like candy—super sweet and not good for you. So here is my attempt to make a less sugar-filled granola with all kinds of healthy seeds and nuts. Pumpkin seeds are loaded with tons of healthy stuff. I won't go into it all, but just Google it, as well as flaxseeds. Feel free to add more dried fruit of your liking or additional nuts and seeds. You can't go too wrong here.

1 Preheat the oven to 300°F. Line two baking sheets with parchment paper.

2 In a large bowl, combine the oats, pumpkin seeds, almonds, pecans, flaxseeds, coconut, brown sugar, cinnamon, and salt. Give it a stir to evenly combine.

3 Put the honey in a small bowl. Microwave for 30 seconds so that it thins out a little. Add the applesauce, coconut oil, and vanilla. Stir to combine. Add the honey mixture to the dry granola mixture and stir well to combine.

4 Spread the granola over the prepared baking sheets and bake for about 1 hour, turning and stirring granola around on the pans every 15 minutes. The baking time may vary a bit, but granola should be a nice dark golden brown when it's ready. "Slow and low" is our granola-baking mantra. Remove from the oven and let the granola cool, then stir in the dried apricots.

5 Enjoy the granola on its own, with your own homemade yogurt, or however you like. Store in a sealed container at room temperature for up to 2 weeks.

NOTE If you add additional dried fruit, stick to ¼ to ½ cup of each and add it at the end. I love cranberries, banana chips, and cherries.

YOGURT PARFAIT

With your favorite fresh fruits, Homemade Yogurt (page 169), and granola, build the easiest, yummiest grab-and-go parfait. Start by placing fresh fruit on the bottom of a jar, top with yogurt, add more fresh fruit, and then top with granola. It is important not to place the granola directly on the yogurt, or it will become super soggy. You can even wrap the granola in plastic and tuck it into the jar on the very top, then just dump it into the fruit and yogurt when you're ready to eat—this keeps the granola super crunchy. I also like to take some twine and tie a spoon around my jar so it truly is ready to eat on the go.

APRICOT-PISTACHIO BREAKFAST BARS

These simple five-ingredient breakfast bars are easy and fun. Apricot and pistachio is one of my fave flavor combos. I can eat a whole bag of dried apricots, so I thought, why not make it a more functional, well-rounded breakfast treat? Dried apricots have lots of health benefits. They are high in antioxidants . . . but mostly high in fiber. You've been warned.

⅔ cup old-fashioned rolled oats

3 tablespoons honey

6 ounces dried apricots (about 1 cup)

¾ cup roasted salted pistachios

⅓ cup white chocolate chips or chopped white chocolate

1   Preheat the oven to 350°F. Line a 9 by 5-inch loaf pan with plastic wrap.

2   Spread the oats over a rimmed baking sheet and lightly toast them in the oven for 3 to 4 minutes. Remove from the oven.

3   Put the honey in a small bowl. Microwave it for about 30 seconds, just so it is more liquid.

4   In a food processor, combine the honey and apricots and process until somewhat smooth but still kinda chunky. Add the toasted oats and pistachios, pulse to combine, and then process until the pistachios are broken down to a crumb-like texture.

5   Firmly press the mixture into the prepared loaf pan liner. Cover with the plastic wrap, then refrigerate for 2 to 3 hours.

6   Remove from the fridge and cut into 5 equal pieces, each about 1¾ by 5 inches.

7   Melt the white chocolate. Drizzle the bars with the melted white chocolate and let the chocolate set. Store the bars in an airtight container at room temperature for up to 1 week or in the fridge for up to 2 weeks.

PREP TIME: 5 minutes   **TOTAL TIME:** 1 hour 10 minutes   **YIELD:** 5 bars

BUZZING BREAKFAST DATE BARS

I am obsessed with these bars. The sweetness from the dates and the soft chewy consistency they bring to the recipe are just delish. The espresso gives you buzz and good flavor. These are hearty, healthy, and filling.

3 tablespoons warm water

2 teaspoons instant espresso powder (I prefer Medaglia d'Oro)

1 cup shredded coconut, sweetened or unsweetened

1 cup packed pitted dates

¾ cup slivered almonds, lightly toasted

¼ cup chopped dried banana (not banana chips)

¼ teaspoon fine sea salt

1 cup old-fashioned rolled oats

½ cup chocolate chips

1 Line a 9 by 5-inch loaf pan with plastic wrap.

2 In a small bowl, combine the water and espresso powder and stir to dissolve the espresso. In a food processor, combine the espresso mixture, coconut, dates, almonds, banana, and salt. Process until the mixture is somewhat smooth. Add the oats and pulse just to combine.

3 Pack the mixture evenly into the prepared loaf pan. Cover and refrigerate for 1 hour.

4 Remove from the fridge and slice into bars.

5 Melt the chocolate chips. Drizzle the bars with the melted chocolate and let the chocolate set. Store in an airtight container in the fridge for up to 1 week.

Berry Delicious
Breakfast Bars, *page 174*

Apricot-Pistachio
Breakfast Bars, *page 171*

Buzzing Breakfast
Date Bars, *opposite*

BERRY DELICIOUS BREAKFAST BARS

Okay, so I'm going to be honest—these bars are essentially dessert. It's basically cobbler in the form of a bar you can eat on the run. Not everything needs to be super healthy, right?! Dessert or not, I love these with coffee in the morning, or really any time of day. I usually wake up to find half the pan gone in the morning, some mystery monster having scavenged them in the night. . . .

CRUST

2 cups old-fashioned rolled oats

1 cup whole wheat flour

1 cup packed dark brown sugar

½ teaspoon ground cinnamon

½ teaspoon ground ginger

¼ teaspoon baking soda

½ teaspoon fine sea salt

¾ cup (1½ sticks) unsalted butter, melted

FILLING

12 ounces fresh raspberries

6 ounces fresh blueberries

6 ounces fresh blackberries

1 peach, pitted and cut into small pieces

½ teaspoon lemon zest

2 teaspoons fresh lemon juice

1 teaspoon vanilla extract

½ cup granulated sugar

2 tablespoons all-purpose flour

CRUMBLE

¼ cup granulated sugar

2 tablespoons unsalted butter, cubed and chilled

½ cup old-fashioned rolled oats

¼ cup all-purpose flour

⅛ teaspoon ground cinnamon

¼ teaspoon fine sea salt

1 **To make the crust:** Preheat the oven to 350°F.

2 In a food processor, combine all the crust ingredients and pulse until combined.

3 Firmly press the crust mixture into an even layer over the bottom of an 8 by 13-inch or similar size baking dish. Bake for 10 minutes, then remove from the oven.

4 **To make the filling:** While the crust is baking, wash and drain the raspberries, blueberries, and blackberries. You don't have to dry them completely. In a large bowl, stir together the berries, peach, lemon zest, lemon juice, vanilla, granulated sugar, and flour.

5 **To make the crumble:** In a food processor, combine all the crumble ingredients. Pulse until the butter is broken down into pea-size pieces.

6 Evenly spread the filling over the baked crust. Spread the crumble evenly over the fruit filling.

7 Bake for 30 to 40 minutes, until the sides are super bubbly and sticky looking and the crumble is lightly golden. Let cool and cut into bars. Store bars in an airtight container at room temperature for 2 days or in the fridge for up to 1 week.

TRAIL MIX BREAKFAST BARS

This is a more manageable option than a loose trail mix when you're literally *on* the trail.

½ cup cashews, toasted

½ cup roasted salted peanuts

¼ cup sweetened shredded coconut

2 heaping tablespoons dried cranberries

2 heaping tablespoons raisins

¼ cup banana chips

3 tablespoons honey

2 heaping tablespoons chocolate chips or mini M&M's

1 Line a 9 by 5-inch loaf pan with plastic wrap.

2 In a food processor, combine the cashews, peanuts, coconut, cranberries, raisins, and banana chips.

3 Put the honey in a small bowl. Microwave for about 30 seconds, just so it is more liquid. Pour the honey over the mixture in the food processor. Pulse a few times until the nuts are just broken up into smaller chunks and the mixture comes together. You don't want it too finely ground—you still want to see hearty chunks of the nuts.

4 Firmly press the mixture evenly into the prepared loaf pan. Sprinkle the chocolate chips over the top and firmly press them into the mixture. Cover and refrigerate for 1 to 2 hours.

5 Remove from the fridge and cut into 5 equal bars. Wrap the bars individually in wax paper, as they are a bit sticky. Store in an airtight container at room temperature for 5 to 7 days or in the fridge for up to 1 week.

KITCHEN SINK FRUIT AND NUT BARS

You can substitute any nuts or fruits you prefer for these anything-goes bars, just make sure to keep the same amounts or you will have to adjust the amount of honey you use.

½ cup coarsely chopped walnuts

½ cup coarsely chopped almonds

½ cup coarsely chopped cashews

¼ cup coarsely chopped pumpkin seeds

¼ cup coarsely chopped dried pineapple

¼ cup coarsely chopped dried apple

½ cup unsweetened shredded coconut

2 teaspoons flaxseeds

¼ teaspoon fine sea salt

⅓ cup honey, warmed

1   Preheat the oven to 350°F. Line an 8-inch square baking dish with parchment paper, allowing the parchment to overhang the edges of the dish (this will allow for easy removal).

2   In a large bowl, combine the walnuts, almonds, cashews, pumpkin seeds, dried pineapple, dried apple, coconut, flaxseeds, and salt. Pour the warmed honey over all and stir until mixed and everything is coated with honey.

3   Press the mixture evenly into the prepared baking dish and bake for 10 to 15 minutes, just until it starts to look lightly golden. Don't overbake, as it will become chewier and the nuts will overroast, giving the bars a slightly bitter, burnt taste.

4   Remove from the oven and let cool slightly in the baking dish, then turn it out onto a cutting board and cut it into 2 by 4-inch bars. Wrap the bars individually in wax paper or put them in an airtight container and store at room temperature for up to 1 week.

NOTE   You can use whatever size baking dish you have, but keep in mind that you might need to double or otherwise adjust the recipe. The bars should be about ½ inch thick.

YOGURT, BARS, BREAKFAST POPS, SMOOTHIES & OTHER HEALTHY YUMS

GREEK YOGURT–RASPBERRY POPS

These creamy, fruity, tangy pops are just like eating a fruit-filled frozen yogurt cup! Breakfast made fun.

1 cup full-fat Greek yogurt or Homemade Yogurt (page 169)

¾ cup simple syrup (recipe follows)

¼ cup whole milk

¼ teaspoon xanthan gum (see sidebar)

6 ounces fresh raspberries (¾ to 1 cup)

1 In a medium bowl, whisk together the yogurt, simple syrup, milk, and xanthan gum until combined. Add the raspberries and stir to combine, breaking up the raspberries into pieces but leaving some big chunks.

2 Pour the mixture into ice pop molds and freeze overnight or for at least 8 hours, following the mold instructions.

A NOTE ABOUT XANTHAN GUM

Don't get freaked out here. Xanthan gum is widely used as a thickener, stabilizer, and emulsifier, and is used in such small amounts in these recipes, you won't even taste it. You can find it at most supermarkets—I love Bob's Red Mill brand. I was first introduced to this ingredient while working at The Bazaar by José Andrés. It has an abundance of uses and can help you achieve some pretty cool stuff in the kitchen. For our purposes, it prevents the ice pops from getting too icy as they freeze, which can happen when you use minimal sugar in your pops, as I do. You don't have to use the xanthan gum, but just know that your pops will be a little bit icier without it unless you increase the sugar content.

PREP TIME: 1 minute   TOTAL TIME: 4 minutes   YIELD: 2 cups simple syrup

SIMPLE SYRUP

1 cup sugar

1 cup water

In a small pot, combine the sugar and water and bring to a boil. Boil for 3 minutes. Let the syrup cool, then store it in an airtight container to use as needed. It will keep in the fridge for 2 to 3 weeks.

Coconut and Matcha Pops, *page 181*

Greek Yogurt–Raspberry Pops, *page 178*

Carrot-Coconut Pops, *page 181*

Thai Iced Tea Pops, *page 183*

COCONUT AND MATCHA POPS

1 cup full-fat Greek yogurt

1 cup canned full-fat coconut milk

2 tablespoons matcha powder

¼ teaspoon ground ginger

¾ cup simple syrup (page 178)

½ teaspoon xanthan gum (see page 178)

I love matcha, and these ice pops will give you just the healthy and filling buzz you need for the day. Balancing the matcha flavor can be tricky—sometimes too much tastes grassy or even fishy. The yogurt and sweetness, though, lend themselves nicely to leave you with a nice earthy and delicious matcha tea flavor.

1   In a blender, combine all the ingredients and blend until combined.

2   Pour the mixture into ice pop molds and freeze overnight or for at least 8 hours, following the mold instructions.

CARROT-COCONUT POPS

1 cup fresh carrot juice

¾ cup canned full-fat coconut milk

¼ cup simple syrup (page 178)

½ teaspoon xanthan gum (see page 178)

These healthy and yummy ice pops are a great way for anybody to get their veggies in. I legitimately love having these for breakfast. They are refreshing, and they pack in all the good nutrients from the carrots. One of these babies gets my morning going for sure.

1   In a medium bowl, whisk together all ingredients until well combined and the xanthan gum has dissolved.

2   Let the mixture sit for 15 minutes, then pour it into ice pop molds and freeze overnight or for at least 8 hours, following the mold instructions.

PEANUT BUTTER–BANANA POPS

1 cup whole milk

2 ripe bananas

¼ cup creamy peanut butter

2 tablespoons sugar

¼ teaspoon xanthan gum (see page 178)

Another delicious classic flavor combo. This is a filling and satisfying ice pop, the perfect frozen meal on a stick.

In a blender, combine all the ingredients and blend until combined. Pour the mixture into ice pop molds and freeze overnight or for at least 8 hours, following the ice pop mold instructions.

ORANGE DREAM POPS

½ cup canned full-fat coconut cream or coconut milk

1 cup orange juice

¼ cup sweetened condensed milk

½ teaspoon vanilla extract

½ orange, peeled and sliced into small pieces

Okay, so this one is based on an orange cream or Creamsicle. The delicious vanilla-and-orange creamy goodness makes me feel like a kid again. For my version, I replace half the dairy with canned coconut cream or coconut milk, and I feel the pops freeze better this way, too.

In a medium bowl, combine the coconut milk, orange juice, sweetened condensed milk, and vanilla. Drop a few pieces of orange into the bottom of each ice pop mold and fill the molds with the milk mixture to about ¼ inch from the top. Drop a few more orange pieces into the milk mixture in the molds. Freeze overnight.

THAI ICED TEA POPS

I love Thai iced tea, but for some reason I have always viewed it as a treat or a dessert—probably because it's so sweet. So here is a caffeine kick-start and sweet treat inspired by the delicious drink.

4 black tea bags

2 cups water

2 star anise pods

1 tablespoon cardamom pods

½ teaspoon whole cloves

2 tablespoons whole milk

⅓ cup sweetened condensed milk

1   In a medium pot, combine the tea, water, star anise, cardamom, and cloves. Bring to a boil and boil for 3 minutes. Remove from the heat, cover the pot, and let it sit for 30 minutes. Strain the tea into a large bowl.

2   In a separate small bowl, stir together the whole milk and condensed milk. Set aside 2 tablespoons of the milk mixture and stir the remaining milk mixture into the tea.

3   Pour ½ teaspoon of the reserved milk mixture into the bottom of each ice pop mold and freeze for 30 minutes to 1 hour. Remove the molds from the freezer and fill them with the tea to about ¼ inch from the top. Freeze for about 45 minutes. Remove the pops from the freezer and pour a little more than ½ teaspoon of the reserved milk mixture on top of each. Insert ice pop sticks. It's okay if the milk mixture seeps down into the pops—you want this to happen. It will give you a sweet creamy center. Freeze overnight or for at least 8 hours.

YOGURT, BARS, BREAKFAST POPS, SMOOTHIES & OTHER HEALTHY YUMS

AVOCADO-PINEAPPLE SMOOTHIE

For this recipe, if you don't have any frozen bananas, you can add a small amount of ice instead. Next time, though, I recommend buying a bunch of bananas, letting them get good and brown and ripe, then peeling and freezing them. They're good to always have on hand, and they are the base for most of my smoothies. You can also portion all the ingredients for this smoothie (minus the water) into freezer bags and freeze them to use later. Then when you're ready for a super-satisfying smoothie, all you have to do is dump them into the blender, add water, and blend!

1 very ripe banana, frozen

½ ripe large avocado

1 cup lightly packed spinach

2 cups chopped fresh pineapple

¾ cup water

8 fresh mint leaves

Pinch of lime zest

Juice of ¼ lime

Pinch of fine sea salt
(Yes, salt in your smoothie! It makes all the difference.)

In a blender, combine all the ingredients and blend until smooth.

NOTE   If you like a thinner consistency, you can add a little extra water or some pineapple juice.

BEETS DON'T KILL MY VIBE SMOOTHIE

I like beets, but I don't love them. They've got some funkiness to their flavor and smell. But this smoothie won't kill your vibe—it will enhance and invigorate it. Beets have some pretty kick-ass health benefits. They can lower blood pressure, and they are rich in fiber and vitamin C. The ginger in this recipe is crucial—it helps cut that funky beet vibe. And don't get me started on the benefits of ginger. It helps with nausea, is anti-inflammatory and full of antioxidants, helps cardiovascular health, etc. Be brave, be bold, try this smoothie, and get your beet on.

1 medium beet, cooked and chopped (about ½ cup—I prefer to buy precooked beets)

2 teaspoons ginger juice (see sidebar, page 191)

1 cup frozen mixed berries

1 Honeycrisp apple, cored and chopped

1 tablespoon honey

1 cup cold water

In a blender, combine all the ingredients and blend until smooth.

START YOUR DAY SMOOTHIE

This is the easy, little-bit-of-everything smoothie I make most every morning. It's simple, filling, and healthy. I like to use the "fruit on the bottom" Greek yogurt—it adds a little extra bit of sweetness. You can use any milk or milk alternative instead of water, too.

1 cup frozen mixed berries

1 (5.3-ounce) container fruit-on-the-bottom Greek yogurt

1 ripe banana

Juice of 1 orange

1 tablespoon vanilla protein powder

½ cup water

Handful of fresh spinach (optional)

In a blender, combine all the ingredients and blend until smooth.

CITRUS–PASSION FRUIT JUICE

Who doesn't love freshly squeezed orange juice? This one is pumped up with a variety of other citrus and passion fruit juices. Passion fruit is my obsession and one of my favorite ingredients as a chef. If you can't find fresh passion fruit, you can get juice, concentrate, or purée—just make sure it's 100 percent passion fruit.

2 blood oranges

2 Cara Cara oranges

2 tangelos

1 grapefruit

1 or 2 fresh passion fruits, or 2 tablespoons passion fruit juice, concentrate, or purée

1   If you have a citrus juicer, cut all the oranges, tangelos, and grapefruit in half and juice away. If you are using an all-purpose juicer or blender, remove the peel and pith of the oranges, tangelos, and grapefruit before juicing them.

2   If you are using fresh passion fruit, scoop out the pulp and vigorously stir it into the citrus juice. (I like the crunchy passion fruit seeds, but if you don't, remove the seeds.) If you are using passion fruit juice or purée instead, simply stir it into the juice.

SEIZE THE SQUEEZE

Juicing always seems like a pain in the butt. And I will be honest: it can be. But I still find the juice is worth the squeeze on this one—especially with how expensive juices are these days. A good juicer is not cheap, but is well worth the cost. I love my Breville juicer. I like to help my juicer out and think I am extending its life a little by chopping my fruit into easier-to-manage pieces before juicing. I don't peel apples, carrots, or peaches before I juice them. A lot of the good stuff is in the peel, so keep it when you can. But for certain fruits and veggies with tougher skins, such as ginger and cooked beets, it's best to peel them first. If you are juicing a lot of stuff, stop and clean out the juicer periodically. If all the leftover bits pile up, it will diminish the juicer's power and keep some of the juice and good nutrients from getting to you. My biggest must-do when juicing is to wrap plastic wrap around the spout and container where the juice is collected—juicing is messy, and this trick will keep you from having to sponge off your walls!

GREEN MACHINE JUICE

I love a green juice! This one is smooth and balanced in flavor and filled with super-healthy ingredients. If this refreshing and delicious juice can't get you to drink your greens, I don't know what will. For those of you with strong feelings about cilantro, rest assured that it's not an overpowering flavor in this smoothie. Still, if you've got *really* strong feelings about cilantro, just leave it out.

2 cups packed, stemmed kale

2 cups packed spinach

2 cups chopped cucumber

1 Golden Delicious apple, cored

1 Fuji apple, cored

1 tablespoon fresh tarragon leaves

½ cup chopped fresh cilantro

½ cup fresh mint leaves

1 In a large bowl, combine all the ingredients. Place the mixture in the juicer. (It is important to combine all the ingredients first, as some of the smaller greens like tarragon and cilantro will just get blown through the juicer if they don't have the bigger items to hold them down.)

2 Drink the juice right away or store it in the fridge in an airtight container for 2 to 3 days. Some separation might occur, so stir well before drinking.

CARROT GINGER TURMERIC JUICE

This super-healthy juice will give you a refreshing boost! Turmeric is an anti-inflammatory and an antioxidant. It's been shown to improve brain function, reduce the pain of arthritis, prevent cancer, and lower the risk of heart disease. Combine the incredible turmeric with the health benefits of ginger and carrot, and you cannot go wrong with this juice.

1½ pounds carrots, washed or peeled

1 palm-size piece fresh ginger, peeled (see sidebar)

½ teaspoon ground turmeric

1　Juice the carrots. Remove the carrots from the juicer and separately juice the the ginger (this should yield 1½ to 2 tablespoons ginger juice—I like this drink spicy!).

2　In a pitcher, stir together the carrot juice, ginger juice, and turmeric. Pour into a glass (or divide between two glasses) and enjoy.

A NOTE ABOUT GINGER JUICE

Ginger is kind of a pain in the butt to juice, but *sooo* worth it. Juice a bunch of ginger and freeze the juice so you always have it on hand. I like to freeze mine in small glass jars (being sure to leave at least ½ inch of space at the top to allow room for expansion). When I'm ready to use it, I pop a jar into the microwave to defrost it, use what I need, and refreeze any that's left. If you don't have a juicer, you can buy ginger juice at Whole Foods or similar stores, or online. Or you can try to snag some from your local juice/smoothie shop. Take a shot of ginger juice to wake your whole body—it's a rush! Perfect way to start the day.

AÇAI BOWL

These super-antioxidant-filled bowls are one of my faves, especially on hot summer days. They make a great breakfast, but I usually enjoy them for lunch or a midafternoon snack. They're a perfect post-workout meal. Top the bowl with any garnishes you like. Get creative, have fun—you can't really go wrong here.

1 cup frozen mixed berries

1 ripe banana

1 cup frozen mango

1 cup chopped fresh pineapple

Juice of 1 orange

1 (3.5-ounce) packet frozen unsweetened açai

1 to 2 tablespoons water

GARNISHES

½ to 1 banana, depending on how hungry you are, sliced

½ cup sliced fresh strawberries

½ cup granola, store-bought or homemade (page 170)

Shredded coconut, sweetened or unsweetened

Goji berries

Any toppings you prefer

1 In a blender, combine the mixed berries, ripe banana, mango, pineapple, orange juice, and açai. Blend, slowly adding the water. The trick here is to keep it very thick, *not* like a smoothie (see Note).

2 Transfer the mixture to a bowl. Top with the sliced banana, strawberries, granola, and a sprinkle of shredded coconut and goji berries. (Or feel free to top it with anything you like!)

NOTE If your blender came with a tamper (that plastic stick that goes through the center of the lid), use it. It'll help you stir the mixture safely so everything blends and stays thick without you having to add too much water.

BAKED APPLE MAPLE OATMEAL

Baked oatmeal is one of my faves. It is so easy, and the possibilities of flavors and fruits and nuts to add are endless, so don't be afraid to experiment. Bake this recipe ahead of time and have it in the fridge. Microwave a bowl, and you have a warm, satisfying breakfast in a minute—literally! This one is particularly delicious. It has a custardy, almost bread pudding–like consistency, and I have even been known to top it with sliced fruit like nectarines, add some vanilla ice cream, and serve it for dessert.

2 cups old-fashioned rolled oats

¾ cup chopped walnuts

1 teaspoon ground ginger

½ teaspoon baking soda

⅓ cup raisins

¾ teaspoon fine sea salt

1¼ teaspoons ground cinnamon

2½ cups chopped peeled Honeycrisp apples

4 tablespoons (½ stick) unsalted butter, melted

1 large egg

2 cups whole milk, at room temperature

½ cup maple syrup

1 teaspoon vanilla extract

1 teaspoon maple extract

1   Preheat the oven to 350°F. Grease a 7½ by 12-inch or similar size baking dish.

2   In a large bowl, stir together the oats, walnuts, ginger, baking soda, raisins, salt, and ¾ teaspoon of the cinnamon until combined.

3   Place the chopped apples in a separate large bowl. Sprinkle 2 tablespoons of the melted butter and the remaining ½ teaspoon cinnamon over the apples and stir to coat the apples.

4   Spread the apples evenly over the bottom of the prepared baking dish.

5   In a separate medium bowl, stir together the egg, milk, maple syrup, vanilla, maple extract, and remaining 2 tablespoons melted butter until combined.

6   Add the egg mixture to the oat mixture and stir to combine, then pour it over the apples, making sure it is evenly distributed. Bake for 30 to 40 minutes, until the center is set.

VEGAN CHAI BLUEBERRY BANANA BAKED OATMEAL

This delicious oatmeal is for all my vegan friends! There's no actual tea in the recipe, but it does have the yummy spices that make a good cup of chai.

1 large banana, sliced

2 cups old-fashioned rolled oats

¼ cup packed dark brown sugar

½ teaspoon baking soda

½ teaspoon ground cardamom

¼ teaspoon ground ginger

Pinch of ground cinnamon

Pinch of freshly ground black pepper

½ teaspoon fine sea salt

6 ounces fresh blueberries (¾ to 1 cup)

¼ cup coconut oil, melted

2 cups coconut milk from a carton, at room temperature

1 teaspoon vanilla extract

1 Preheat the oven to 350°F. Grease a 7½ by 12-inch or similar size baking dish.

2 Arrange the banana slices evenly over the bottom of the prepared baking dish.

3 In a large bowl, stir together the oats, brown sugar, baking soda, cardamom, ginger, cinnamon, pepper, salt, and blueberries until combined.

4 In a separate medium bowl, stir together the coconut oil, coconut milk, and vanilla until combined. Add the coconut mixture to the oatmeal mixture and stir to combine, then pour it over the bananas, making sure the mixture is evenly distributed. Bake for 30 to 35 minutes, until the center is set.

TRAIL MIX

I am a huge snacker, and I love a salty-sweet combo, so trail mix is my jam. It's a filling snack and a good pick-me-up. I hike a lot, and this snack gets its name for a reason. I like to use mini M&M's in mine because they make it colorful and fun, and that candy coating prevents melting when you're on summer hikes.

1 cup cashews, toasted

1 cup roasted salted peanuts

½ cup sweetened shredded coconut

⅓ cup raisins

¼ cup dried cranberries, unsweetened

⅓ cup mini M&M's or chocolate chips

½ cup banana chips

In a large bowl, combine all the ingredients. Store the trail mix in an airtight container at room temperature for up to 2 weeks.

MANGO-RASPBERRY FRUIT LEATHER

A homemade fruit roll-up is so much better than the store-bought kind, and with *sooo* much less added sugar. The kiddos and adults will love this inexpensive and easy at-home version—it's too easy not to do. Have fun and experiment with different fruit flavors, adding as much or as little sugar as you want. Strawberry works great, too, or try strawberry mixed with blackberries.

1 large ripe mango, peeled and chopped

6 ounces fresh raspberries

2 tablespoons sugar

1   Preheat the oven to 150°F. Line a rimmed 12½ by 17¼-inch (half-sheet) pan with a silicone baking mat.

2   In a blender or food processor, blend the mango until smooth. Transfer the mango to a bowl and set it aside. Add the raspberries and sugar to the blender and blend until smooth. (It is important to blend the raspberries with the sugar, as the sugar helps liquefy the berries.)

3   Place dollops of the mango and raspberry purées on the prepared pan. With a small offset spatula, spread the purées evenly over the pan—try to spread them as evenly as possible, not too thin and not too thick, and try not to spread them to the very edges, so you'll have room to grab the fruit leather and peel it off the mat when it's cool.

4   Bake for 2 hours 30 minutes to 3 hours, rotating the baking sheet every hour. The leather is done when it is still tacky but not too sticky or wet. Let the leather cool.

5   Remove it from the mat and place it on top of a sheet of wax paper. Cut the leather and wax paper into strips with scissors and roll them up paper-side out, then store them in a sealed container at room temperature for up to 1 week.

BOOZY DAYTIME ADVENTURES

WATERMELON-JALAPEÑO SMASH

This drink is perfect for the margarita bar (page 208), but it also works great with vodka. Pick your poison and have fun. This is definitely not on the spicy side of things. It has a nice jalapeño flavor and a *little* spice, but I am not trying to set anybody on fire early in the day. If you do want to go for it, add all the extra jalapeño you can handle. Using fresh pieces of watermelon gives this drink a thicker, fresher consistency that I love.

6 (1-inch) cubes fresh watermelon

1½ ounces tequila or vodka

4 (⅛-inch-thick) slices jalapeño

1½ teaspoons simple syrup (page 178)

Squeeze of fresh lime juice

Ice cubes

Combine all the ingredients in a shaker with your preferred amount of ice. Shake, pour into a tumbler or old-fashioned glass, and drink.

BAR NOTES

My recs for wallet-friendly but good booze: Espolòn Reposado tequila and Tito's vodka.

THYME-PEACH TEA SMASH

This fruity jazzed-up tea reminds me of my favorite Snapple flavor, peach iced tea. It's been a while since I've actually *had* a Snapple, but I still remember that delicious flavor combo. Feel free to make the virgin version of this for a super-refreshing, fun iced tea.

½ cup boiling water

1 black tea bag

½ teaspoon fresh lemon juice

1 tablespoon simple syrup (page 178)

Leaves from 1 large sprig thyme, plus a sprig for garnish

¼ peach, cubed, plus a slice for garnish

1 to 1½ ounces rye whiskey (depending on how boozy you want it)

Cinnamon stick

Ice cubes

1   In a glass measuring cup, combine the boiling water and the tea bag, and set aside to steep for at least 3 minutes.

2   In a cocktail shaker, combine the lemon juice, simple syrup, thyme, peach, whiskey, cinnamon stick, and ¼ cup of the brewed tea. Add your preferred amount of ice and shake well.

3   Remove the cinnamon stick and dump the entire contents of the shaker into a highball glass. Garnish with a sprig of thyme and a slice of peach.

PREP TIME: 3 minutes   *TOTAL TIME:* 3 minutes   *YIELD:* Makes 1 cocktail

THE PURE AND SIMPLE MARGARITA

I like my margaritas pure and simple, as the name suggests. This margarita is tart and tequila-forward, not too sweet, but feel free to adjust the sweetness to your liking.

Coarse salt, for the rim of the glass

Lime wedge, for the rim of the glass

Ice cubes

3 tablespoons fresh lime juice

2 tablespoons simple syrup (page 178)

1½ ounces tequila

Squeeze of fresh orange juice (about ½ teaspoon)

1   Pour some salt onto a small, shallow plate. Run the lime wedge around the rim of a margarita glass or preferred glass and dip the rim into the salt to coat.

2   In a shaker filled with ice, combine the lime juice, simple syrup, tequila, and orange juice. Shake, pour into the prepared glass, and drink.

PASSION FRUIT MARGARITA

It is no secret that I love anything passion fruit! It is my all-time favorite flavor. It is also no secret that I love margaritas, so this is the perfect marriage of my favorite things.

Ice cubes

2 tablespoons passion fruit purée (see Note)

2½ tablespoons simple syrup (page 178)

1½ ounces tequila

Fresh passion fruit and seeds, for garnish (optional)

Coarse salt or sweet salt (page 209) for the rim (optional)

In a cocktail shaker filled with ice, combine the passion fruit purée, simple syrup, and tequila. Shake, pour into a margarita glass or preferred glass, garnish with passion fruit and seeds, and dip the glass rim in salt, if desired, and serve.

NOTE   Passion fruit purée and juice can be hard to find in stores, so I order the purée online. I like to use purée, as it is pure passion fruit, therefore stronger in flavor than juice. If you are using juice, which is more readily available, be careful with the sweetness. Juices usually have added sugar, so you may not need to use the simple syrup, or you may need to add up to double the amount of juice for a good strong passion fruit flavor.

MARGARITA BAR

This is one of my favorite additions to a brunch or a Cinco de Mayo celebration. I set up a table with all the margarita options, garnishes, and tequila and let my guests create their own drinks. I even like to tell them to bring their favorite bottle of tequila to share—that way, the margarita bar gets even more fun and you get to try all the different kinds of tequila, too. Note that some of these work best when made the night before.

PITCHER-SIZE MARGARITA BLENDS

These margarita blends make a full pitcher, for mixing and matching with different tequilas and garnishes.

CLASSIC MARGARITA

Combine 2 cups fresh lime juice (from 16 to 18 limes) with 1¼ to 1½ cups simple syrup (page 178)—you may want to start with 1 cup simple syrup and then add more to your taste.

GRAPEFRUIT-MINT MARGARITA

Combine 2 cups grapefruit juice with 5 large sprigs mint, gently twisting the mint sprigs before adding them to the grapefruit juice. This one is best when you make it the night before and store it in the fridge to let the flavors combine.

PASSION FRUIT MARGARITA

Combine 1¼ cups passion fruit purée, 1¼ to 1¾ cups simple syrup (page 178), and ¾ cup water. Start with 1¼ cups of the syrup and add more to taste. (If using passion fruit juice instead of purée, do not add the water.)

WATERMELON-JALAPEÑO MARGARITA

Combine 2 cups watermelon juice with 1 sliced fresh jalapeño and refrigerate overnight before serving. Taste it the next day and add more watermelon juice or jalapeño to reach your desired level of spiciness.

MARGARITA SALT

In addition to plain salt for rimming the glasses, try these combinations:

LIME SALT

Combine 2 tablespoons coarse salt with 1 to 2 teaspoons lime zest. This is best made ahead of time and covered with plastic.

SWEET AND SOUR

Add a little sugar to Lime Salt.

SWEET SALT

Combine 2 tablespoons coarse salt with 1 tablespoon sugar.

TAJÍN SEASONING

Run a lime wedge around the rim of the glass and dip the rim into Tajín to coat.

GARNISHES

Mint leaves
Lime twists

Slices of lemon, lime, and grapefruit
Sliced jalapeños

Fresh passion fruit
Fruit- or flower-filled ice cubes

Slices of fresh watermelon
Tonic water to add fizz to Classic Margarita

HIBISCUS-LIME COOLER

Hibiscus is a fun and exotic flavor you don't see too much. I love it for its gorgeous color and flavor. This is a fun, tart, and refreshing beverage that looks as beautiful as it tastes.

1 tablespoon dried hibiscus leaves, plus more for garnish

1 cup boiling water

1 tablespoon fresh lime juice

1½ tablespoons simple syrup (page 178)

1 ounce ginger beer

1½ ounces spiced rum

Ice cubes

Lime twist, for garnish

1   In a glass measuring cup, combine the hibiscus leaves and the boiling water and set aside to steep for 3 minutes. Strain the hibiscus tea and set aside to cool.

2   In a shaker, combine the lime juice, simple syrup, ginger beer, rum, and ¼ cup of the cooled hibiscus tea. Shake and pour into a glass over ice. Garnish with a hibiscus leaf and the lime twist.

THE STANDARD

I was first introduced to a version of this cocktail at SoHo House. Theirs was made with gin, and they called it the Eastern Standard. I was obsessed at first sip, so I set out into the world to order this drink everywhere I went. To my surprise, nobody had heard of it. Google the ingredients, and there are tons of variations, but it doesn't seem to have a "standard" name, if you will. So I call my version The Standard, since it was just that at my house for a while. Mine is made with vodka, as I'm not much of a gin drinker, and like most of my drinks, it is not so sweet the way a lot of restaurant-style drinks out there tend to be. It is invigorating, tangy, minty fresh, and delicious all the way around.

6 (⅛- to ¼-inch-thick) slices cucumber

5 or 6 large mint leaves, plus 1 leaf for garnish

Juice of ½ lime

Ice cubes

1 tablespoon simple syrup (page 178)

1½ ounces vodka

In a cocktail shaker, combine 5 slices of the cucumber, the mint leaves, and the lime juice and muddle well. Add your preferred amount of ice, simple syrup, and vodka. Shake well and strain into a shallow glass. Garnish with the remaining cucumber slice and mint leaf.

CHAI TODDY

I love a hot toddy. It's warm, comforting, sweet, tangy, and boozy. What's not to love? I wanted to jazz it up with chai, but you can use regular black tea or chamomile tea, or even replace the tea with plain hot water. This does work cold over ice, too! Just brew the tea, add the honey while it's hot, and then chill.

1 cup boiling water

1 chai tea bag

2 teaspoons fresh lemon juice

3½ teaspoons honey

1 ounce bourbon

½ ounce spiced rum

Lemon twist, for garnish

Cinnamon stick, for garnish

In a mug, combine the boiling water and tea bag and set aside to steep for 1 minute. Remove the tea bag and add the lemon juice and honey. Stir to combine. Add the bourbon and spiced rum, and stir. Garnish with the lemon twist and cinnamon stick and enjoy!

BRUNCH PUNCH

This is a delicious, refreshing, bright, and super-fun brunch punch that's festive enough for any occasion. I make this all the time! It's even good to take to a party—just use a pitcher with a lid or cover it with plastic, and voilà! In a punch bowl, it's the perfect colorful centerpiece for any table spread.

1 bottle prosecco brut

2 cups Lillet

¾ cup pineapple juice

2 tablespoons simple syrup (page 178)

¼ cup unsweetened cranberry juice

½ cup ginger ale

4 large strawberries, sliced

3 slices orange

8 fresh mint leaves

½ Honeycrisp apple, cored and sliced

Combine all ingredients in a punch bowl or pitcher and stir to combine. Add large pieces of ice or an ice block, if using a punch bowl.

SPARKLING BLUEBERRIES

Add these to champagne, Brunch Punch (above), mimosas, or any drink that could use some sparkle! You'll need a whipped cream dispenser. My favorite brand is iSi. To make whipped cream, these dispensers or canisters use N_2O chargers, but we want to sparkle, not whip! So instead of using N_2O chargers, use CO_2 chargers that you'd use to make soda water.

Put 1 to 2 inches of blueberries in the bottom of your whipped cream dispenser (that's about ½ cup blueberries, depending on the size of your dispenser). Close the dispenser and add two CO_2 soda chargers according to your dispenser's instructions. Refrigerate for at least 4 to 6 hours, or up to overnight. *Before* you open the dispenser, be sure to expel all the gas from the canister with the nozzle. This is very important so that it won't explode in your face. Carefully open the dispenser and enjoy your blueberries. They won't stay sparkly for very long, so use what you need and keep the container sealed.

BOOZY SOAKED FRUIT

The sky is the limit here. You can get as creative as you want. You can soak pineapple in rum for a piña colada–inspired flavor. Soak strawberries in champagne. Put watermelon, other melons, and berries in vodka. Have fun with this one. As a rule of thumb, I like to place my fruit in a shallow, wider-bottomed dish, then pour over the alcohol to just cover the fruit. Cover and refrigerate for anywhere from 4 to 24 hours. Drain off the booze and store the fruit in the fridge to use in mixed drinks. It's fun to set out bowls of these on their own on your brunch table, but be sure to let your guests know they are for the 21+ crowd only! They are great to use as garnishes in mimosas, plain champagne, or any other drink. Skewer them for fun kebabs. I'm gonna let you do your thing with this one.

BREAKFAST BUBBLY

I always use a dry champagne for mimosas rather than a sweet one, since you are adding sweet juices to it. The dry champagne creates a better balance and won't leave you with an overly sweet drink (or as much of a headache later!). Also, unless it's a special celebration, I will use cava or prosecco instead of true champagne—making me and my wallet happy, thus making me pour more bubbles!

PREP TIME: 1 minute   **TOTAL TIME**: 1 minute   **YIELD**: Makes 1 cocktail

CLASSIC MIMOSA

Brunch isn't brunch without mimosas. Here is the classic mimosa recipe, a staple that never goes out of style. I always say, if it ain't broke, don't fix it.

¼ cup fresh orange juice

¾ cup champagne, cava, or prosecco

Pour the orange juice into a champagne glass, then add the champagne. Voilà.

Grapefruit-Mint Mimosa, *page 218*

Raspberry-Rose Mimosa, *page 219*

Classic Mimosa, *opposite*

GRAPEFRUIT-MINT MIMOSA

I love grapefruit juice, and paired with mint, it goes well with any alcohol. I use this combo with vodka, with tequila, and, of course, with champagne.

3 tablespoons fresh
grapefruit juice

3 large fresh mint leaves

¾ cup champagne, cava,
or prosecco

Pour the grapefruit juice into a champagne glass. Give a gentle twist to the mint leaves to open up their flavor and add them to the glass. Top with the champagne.

RASPBERRY-ROSE MIMOSA

I am not one to normally enjoy things made with rose water, or to make them myself. The flavor can be really overpowering and make you feel like you just drank Grandma's perfume. In this mimosa, however, I find it to be just subtle enough while adding a fun twist.

⅛ teaspoon rose water

½ teaspoon simple syrup (page 178)

1 tablespoon cranberry juice

4 fresh raspberries

¾ cup champagne, cava, or prosecco

Food-grade rose petal, for garnish (optional)

In a champagne flute, combine the rose water, simple syrup, cranberry juice, and raspberries. Very gently, so that you don't break the glass, break up the raspberries with a spoon or fork. Add the champagne and garnish with a rose petal, if desired.

MIMOSA BAR

JUICES
Display carafes of fresh orange juice, cranberry juice, grapefruit juice, or any other juices you like.

BUBBLIES
Keep bottles of champagne, cava, and/or prosecco in ice buckets on the table.

GIFTS
Have fun gifts like little potted plants for your guests to take away. Think lavender potted plants if you're hosting the Fancy Parisian Gathering (see page 234).

ICE
Keep buckets of ice nearby and don't leave everything out for too long. Nothing worse than a warm mimosa!

GARNISHES

Put out bowls of sliced strawberries, raspberries, blueberries, Boozy Soaked Fruit (see page 214), and Sparkling Blueberries (see page 214).

Have a colorful collection of oranges, limes, and lemons with peelers close by so guests can make fun garnishes.

Display fresh edible flowers, such as pansies, sprigs of lavender, rose petals, and violets. (Be sure to purchase flowers that are marked as "edible" or "food-grade" and that come from a trusted source.)

Put edible flowers and/or Boozy Soaked Fruit (see page 214) in the wells of an ice cube tray and fill the wells with distilled water to make fabulous ice cubes—distilled water is key, as it freezes clear!

BLOODY MARY

I must admit, I was never a huge Bloody Mary fan. Something about tomato juice and booze always turned me off. My mom *was* a huge fan, though, so I grew up eating her celery garnish, and that was about all the taste I acquired. (Yes, my mother let her young daughter eat her vodka-soaked celery, and I still thank her for it to this day!) I decided to set out to make a damn good Bloody Mary that my mom and I could both enjoy. I bought a smorgasbord of ingredients based on the zillion possibilities and recipes I found on the internet, but in the end, I settled on this classic with a little kick—celery garnish included!

SALT RIM

2 teaspoons coarse salt

½ teaspoon plus ⅛ teaspoon celery salt

⅛ teaspoon onion powder

¼ teaspoon smoked paprika

Lime wedge

BLOODY MARY MIX

½ cup tomato juice (I prefer V8)

8 drops of Tabasco sauce

1 teaspoon prepared horseradish

½ teaspoon Worcestershire sauce

⅛ teaspoon celery salt

⅛ teaspoon onion powder

Juice of ½ lemon

Pinch of freshly ground black pepper

½ teaspoon finely chopped jarred pepperoncini, plus ¾ teaspoon pickling brine from the jar

2 pinches of fine sea salt

½ teaspoon brown sugar

ASSEMBLY

3 ounces vodka (I prefer Tito's)

Ice cubes

2 celery stalks, for garnish

2 whole pickled pepperoncini, for garnish

1   **To make the salt rim:** Combine all the ingredients except the lime wedge in a small bowl. Rub the lime wedge over the rim of a glass, then dip the rim into the salt mixture to coat. Repeat to coat the rim of a second glass.

2   **To make the Bloody Mary mix:** Combine all the ingredients in a cocktail shaker. Shake well.

3   **To serve:** Add the vodka to the shaker with the Bloody Mary mix and shake well to combine.

4   Fill the prepared glasses with your preferred amount of ice and divide the Bloody Mary between them. Garnish with the celery and whole pepperoncini, or as desired.

MICHELADA

This is a classic Mexican cocktail—think Bloody Mary with beer. I was skeptical at first, as I have a natural aversion to tomato juice, but I'm sold. You get the refreshing qualities of beer with a savory flavor that is oh so good.

Tajín seasoning, for the rim

Lime wedge, for the rim

2 ounces Clamato juice

2 or 3 dashes of Tabasco sauce

1 or 2 dashes of Worcestershire sauce

1 tablespoon fresh lime juice

Dash of soy sauce

1 (12-ounce) beer (I prefer Modelo Especial or Corona)

Spread some Tajín over a small, shallow plate. Run the lime wedge around the rim of a tall glass and dip the rim into the Tajín to coat. Add the Clamato, Tabasco, Worcestershire, lime juice, and soy sauce to the glass. Stir to combine. Top off with the beer, stir again, and enjoy.

SMOKY PARADISE COCKTAIL

This was inspired by a drink I'd had and loved, but I had no idea what was in it other than grapefruit and mezcal. I had it at a whiskey saloon, so I figured it had to have some whiskey, too. I set out to make my own, and here it is. It's now one of my faves. It's not too smoky since we are going for brunch and day drinking. I find it to have a nice, smoky, sweet, and tart balance.

¼ cup grapefruit juice

1½ tablespoons simple syrup (page 178)

1 ounce mezcal

½ ounce rye whiskey

3 dashes of Angostura bitters

Juice of ½ lime

Ice cubes

Grapefruit twist, for garnish

Combine all the ingredients except the grapefruit twist in a shaker. Shake, pour into a glass, garnish with the grapefruit twist, and enjoy!

BOURBON APPLE CIDER

This is one of my all-time fall favorites. I always have a batch of cider going during the fall. It makes the house smell delicious. The spiced cider is perfect to drink on its own, but when you can add bourbon to something and make it better . . . why not!? I like to fill up mason jars with cider and adorn them with pretty ribbon and fresh cinnamon sticks to pass out as gifts or party favors. You can even add a travel-size bottle of bourbon for the perfect gift.

SPICED APPLE CIDER

6 Fuji apples, cored

4 or 5 cinnamon sticks

1 tablespoon whole cloves

½ cup cubed peeled
fresh ginger

3 large pieces orange zest
(peeled with a vegetable peeler)

2 tablespoons sugar

COCKTAIL

Ice cubes

1½ ounces bourbon (I prefer
Woodford Reserve for
this drink)

Cinnamon stick, for garnish

Orange twist, for garnish

1 **To make the spiced apple cider:** In a large pot, combine all the ingredients and bring to a boil. Boil for 20 to 30 minutes, then reduce the heat to low, cover, and simmer for 1 hour.

2 Mash up the apples in the pot, then cover again and simmer for 2 hours more. Remove from the heat and let cool.

3 Strain the cider through a large fine-mesh sieve into a 2-quart storage container, using a rubber spatula to really mash all the juice out of the apples. The cider will keep in the refrigerator for up to 2 weeks.

4 **To make the cocktail:** In a shaker filled with ice, combine ½ cup of the cider and the bourbon. Shake. Strain into a glass over ice, if desired. Garnish with the cinnamon stick and orange twist.

LEMON SLUSHY FOR ADULTS ONLY

This frozen treat is perfect for those hot summer days! It's boozy yet refreshing, with just the right amount of sour and sweet. These get me every time. They are so good, they go down too easily, and before you know it, the party has started! But worry not—there is coconut water in it, so it is totally hydrating!

¼ cup fresh lemon juice

¼ cup simple syrup (page 178)

¼ cup coconut water

Ice cubes

3 or 4 large fresh mint leaves, plus a sprig for garnish

1½ ounces vodka

Lemon slice, for garnish

In a blender, combine the lemon juice, simple syrup, coconut water, your preferred amount of ice, mint leaves, and vodka and blend until smooth. Pour into a glass, garnish with a fun party straw, the slice of lemon, and the sprig of mint, and drink.

ICED MOCHA AND BAILEYS

This is my new obsession. It is almost dessert-like, and it gives a great buzz. Coffee has gases, so when you shake it up, it gets really frothy. This drink is creamy, chocolaty, boozy, and caffeinated. It's like a milk shake with superpowers.

1 tablespoon half-and-half

Ice cubes

1 teaspoon unsweetened dark cocoa powder

1 teaspoon sugar

½ cup brewed coffee, cold

1½ ounces Baileys Irish Cream

1 Pour the half-and-half into a tall, slender glass.

2 In a cocktail shaker filled with the ice, combine the cocoa powder, sugar, and coffee. Shake. Pour everything into the glass with the half-and-half and top with the Baileys. Stir gently to combine and enjoy!

PARTY MENUS

MOTHER'S DAY BREAKFAST IN BED

Make her morning!

RASPBERRY-ROSE MIMOSA
(page 219)

EGGS BENEDICT with HOLLANDAISE SAUCE (page 47)

GREEK YOGURT–RASPBERRY LOAF (page 121)

SHOW THE LOVE Cut a slice of the raspberry loaf and, with a large heart-shaped cookie cutter, cut it into a heart shape. Add a small vase of her favorite flowers to the breakfast tray, and I think you will have made her morning!

FATHER'S DAY BRUNCH

The essential man brunch!

BLOODY MARYS (page 222)

CHICKEN and WAFFLES (page 76)

BUTTERMILK BISCUITS with HONEY BUTTER (page 97)

FRIED DOUGHNUTS (page 142)

FENNEL SAUSAGE and MUSHROOM QUICHE (page 40)

DAD VIBE Lay out your buffet spread on the coffee table in front of the couch. Invite all the other dads over and put sports on the TV. Let Dad indulge and enjoy.

TAKE-AWAY MAN GIFT Make jars of spiced apple cider (see page 226) with travel-size bottles of bourbon tied to them, or fill small mason jars with Bloody Mary mix (see page 222) and attach travel-size vodka bottles.

BREAKFAST FOR DINNER PARTY

PJ's and slippers required!

MIMOSA BAR (page 221)

ASSORTMENT of SWEET and SAVORY FANCY PASTRIES (pages 139–164)

SWEET POTATO HASH with EGGS (page 54)

SWEET and SAVORY FRENCH TOAST SANDWICHES (pages 81–93)

FRITTATAS (pages 33–36)

BREAKFAST POPS (pages 178–183)

THE KEY HERE IS COMFY, COZY, AND FUN
Pick your favorite breakfast foods to share—the ones I've listed are just suggestions! The Sweet Potato Hash with Eggs is a good dinner option, or you could do Chicken and Waffles (page 76) instead. For the mimosa station, be sure to have buckets of ice and chilled champagne (or other sparkling wine) with plenty of juices and garnishes. Line your table with lots of candles to create a cozy nighttime vibe. I like to keep my oven on at 150ºF, or the lowest temp possible, so I can keep food warm and then replenish the table as needed. Put out small amounts to start and restock as the party goes on.

GOODY BAGS   These are my favorite part! Fill cute colored paper or fabric bags with tissue paper and then add your favorite travel-size goodies, such as little toothbrushes, lotions, mini travel candles, and cute eye pillows—all the slumber and pajama party essentials.

FIESTA PARTY

Hang the *piñata*!

MARGARITA BAR (page 208)

MICHELADAS (page 224)

CHILAQUILES (page 49)

HUEVOS RANCHEROS (page 57)

GALLO PINTO (page 58)

CINNAMON SUGAR–COATED BRIOCHE BEIGNETS (page 139)

FRIED DOUGHNUTS (page 142) **with LIME ZEST SPRINKLED on the VANILLA GLAZE**

QUICK-AND-EASY CENTERPIECE   In a glass bowl or a short, wide glass vase, arrange your favorite combination of citrus fruits, such as limes, lemons, oranges, kumquats, and key limes. The addition of a few smaller types adds a nice texture. Stick a few pieces of greenery or leaves among the fruit, and there you have it!

OVERACHIEVER CENTERPIECE   In a glass vase filled with water, add lots and lots of thick-cut slices of citrus—any citrus fruit or a combination of several is perfect. Then add your flowers as you would in any arrangement, being sure to push the fruit slices against the wall of the vase. I like to use Gerbera daisies or dahlias, which I think work nicely with the citrus. Wildflowers are also lovely, so choose your favorites. The more greenery you add to the flowers, the better, as that naturally ties in the citrus to the flowers.

FANCY PARISIAN GATHERING

Bon appétit!

CLASSIC MIMOSAS (page 216)

BAGUETTE (page 111)
with **APPLE BUTTER** (page 129)
and/or **PEACH-THYME JAM**
(page 125) or **CHERRY–STAR
ANISE JAM** (page 128)

**NUTELLA and BANANA FRENCH
TOAST SANDWICHES** (page 85)

**EGGS BENEDICT WITH
HOLLANDAISE SAUCE** (page 47)

VARIETY of CROISSANTS
(pages 149–152)

**APPLE-ALMOND TART with
ORANGE ESSENCE** (page 157)

*LA SAUCE ET LES
FLEURS*   Eggs Benedict is
technically an American invention,
but hollandaise is one of the five
mother sauces of French cooking,
so do your part for international
relations and enjoy this French
American favorite. Be sure to adorn
your table with lots of irises—the
national flower of France and the
model for the fleur-de-lis, the
emblem of the French crown.

INDEX

Note: Page numbers in *italics* indicate photographs.

IN THIS SERIES

Auto Racing

Baseball

Basketball

Football

Golf

Hockey

Lacrosse

Soccer

Tennis

Track and Field

Wrestling

THE COMPOSITE GUIDE

to **FOOTBALL**

DENNIS TUTTLE

CHELSEA HOUSE PUBLISHERS

Philadelphia

Produced by Choptank Syndicate, Inc.

Editor and Picture Researcher: Norman L. Macht
Production Coordinator and Editorial Assistant: Mary E. Hull
Design and Production: Lisa Hochstein
Cover Illustrator: Cliff Spohn
Cover Design: Keith Trego
Art Director: Sara Davis

First Printing

1 3 5 7 9 8 6 4 2

Library of Congress Cataloging-in-Publication Data

Tuttle, Dennis R.
       The composite guide to football / Dennis Tuttle.
          p.   cm.— (The composite guide)
       Includes bibliographical references (p.) and index.
       Summary: Surveys the history of the sport of football, discussing its somewhat
unclear origins, the evolution of its rules and popularity, and some of the key
players and games.
    ISBN 0-7910-4725-3
    1. National Football League—History—Juvenile literature.
    2. Football—United States—History—Juvenile literature.
[1. Football—History.] I. Title. II. Series.
GV955.5.N35T88 1998
796.332'64'0973'— dc21   97-33538
                                                                  CIP
                                                                  AC

CONTENTS

1 SUNDAYS OF GLORY

For the first half of the 20th century, long before John Madden, the Super Bowl, and the Dallas Cowboys, professional football was a minor part of the American sports scene. Baseball was by far the most popular sport, and even boxing and horse racing got bigger headlines in the newspapers. High school and college football had large followings, but that enthusiasm did not carry over to the pro game. For many years there were just eight to 12 teams in the National Football League. Outside of those cities few people ever saw or cared about the NFL.

All of that changed on December 28, 1958.

On a mild but gray winter day at Yankee Stadium, the New York Giants and Baltimore Colts played for the NFL Championship before a national television audience. It may not seem like such a big deal now, but in those days football was rarely seen on television. A college game might be shown on Saturday, and some NFL teams aired their games on local TV. But few people watched television on Sunday afternoons. It was a day of church, rest, and spending time with your family. The networks wondered if Sunday football games on TV would change viewing habits. With TV sets in nearly two-thirds of American homes, NBC decided to find the answer.

The 1958 NFL Championship has often been called "The Greatest Game Ever Played." The truth is that most of the game lacked drama and

Alan Ameche goes through a big hole in the Giants' line to score the winning touchdown in the Baltimore Colts' 23–17 overtime victory at New York for the NFL Championship on December 28, 1958.

excitement. The Colts had a commanding 14–3 lead in the third period and were driving for another score that would put the game out of reach. They were clearly the better team. With 30 million people watching on TV, one could hear a collective yawn rising.

But at that point the national popularity of pro football and the impact of sports on television officially began. The Giants regrouped and stopped the Colts' drive at the New York 3-yard line. Then the Giants scored two touchdowns to take the lead. Suddenly the nation's viewers edged closer to their TV screens.

Trailing 17–14 with 1:56 to play, no time-outs remaining, and the ball on his own 14-yard line, quarterback Johnny Unitas of the Colts calmly walked into the huddle, snapped on his chin strap, and said to his teammates, "Now we're going to find out what we're made of."

Unitas completed four consecutive passes in a heart-stopping drive that moved the ball to the Giants' 20. With seven seconds remaining, Steve Myhra kicked a field goal that made the score 17–17 and pushed a championship game into overtime for the first time.

Since the title game had never needed an extra period, the TV announcers were confused about the tie-breaking rules. Even the officials had to check the rule book to be sure that the first team to score would be the champions. The Giants won the coin toss and got the first possession. But the Colts' defense held and the Giants were forced to punt, giving the Colts the ball at their own 20-yard line.

Standing 80 yards from glory, the cool Unitas calmly engineered a spectacular 12-play drive. He converted a third-and-14 pass to his best receiver, Raymond Berry, for 20 yards to the Giants' 43. The great quarterback then used a variety of running plays with Alan Ameche and L.G. Dupre, and short passes to Berry and Lenny Moore, to get the ball to the New York 8. During a time-out, Colts coach Weeb Ewbank told Unitas not to throw the ball. "Keep it on the ground," he ordered. But Unitas believed in calling his own plays. He trotted back onto the field and completed a short pass to tight end Jim Mutscheller, who slipped out of bounds at the 1. The 64,185 fans at Yankee Stadium were standing, stomping, and screaming, "Let's go, Giants!" Television viewers sat glued to their sets. The suspense was unbearable when suddenly . . .

The television screen went blank!

Twenty panicked NBC officials rushed from the broadcast booth to help find the problem. In Baltimore, furious fans tossed beer mugs and dishes at their sets and scrambled for their radios. A drunk staggered onto the field, eluding security and delaying the game long enough for Unitas to walk to the sideline and confer with coach Ewbank again. They elected to go for the touchdown rather than a field goal.

As it turned out, the drunk on the field was a perfectly sober NBC executive whose mission had been to delay the game long enough for technicians to fix the problem. They found that a cable had been kicked loose by the excited fans. As Unitas walked up to the line of scrimmage, the TV picture suddenly reappeared.

Unitas had called "16-power," a play in which Ameche would run between the guard and right tackle. At the snap of the ball, Mutscheller, tackle George Preas, and Moore

Johnny Unitas played the entire 1958 championship game wearing a corset of foam rubber and steel to protect three broken ribs. Unitas, who was elected to the Hall of Fame in 1979, led the NFL in passing yardage and touchdowns four times and played in 10 Pro Bowls.

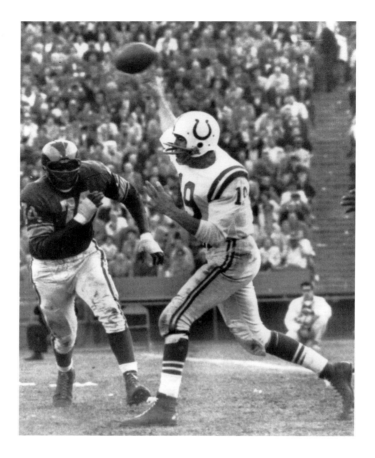

executed their blocks perfectly. Ameche, his head down and both hands on the ball, barreled into the end zone for the 23–17 victory. The first hands to touch him were those of overjoyed Baltimore fans who spilled into the end zone.

The nation was thrilled. For weeks fans all across the country talked about the game. Kids imitated Unitas in backyard games, and for the first time football talk was about the NFL, not the college bowl games. Advertisers sensed the game's appeal, and the public began to look more closely at the Sunday athletes behind the face masks. Pro football stars such as Unitas, Browns fullback Jim Brown, Giants linebacker Sam Huff and halfback Frank Gifford, Packers halfback Paul Hornung, and Rams quarterback Norm Van Brocklin suddenly became household names and heroes, just like baseball stars Ted Williams, Willie Mays, and Mickey Mantle.

The oddity in this new-found attention was that pro football had been blessed with legendary games and players since the first college star was secretly paid to play for a town team in 1892. But without television and the enthusiasm of a national audience sparked by that thrilling conclusion to the 1958 Colts' championship victory, Sunday afternoons for football fans still might not be much different from the turn of the century—when college boys played a game where nobody threw the ball, and only a few of their friends cared enough to watch them play.

FROM SKULLS TO SCRIMMAGES

2

Like most sports, football's origins are difficult to trace. The common belief is that football derived from rugby, which came from soccer. But the roots of soccer are also a mystery. One theory has soccer being played by the ancient Greeks and Romans. The Chinese probably played some form of soccer around 500 A.D.

A widely accepted belief among historians is that sometime around 1050, English workmen clearing out an old battlefield found the skull of a Danish invader. To show their ill feelings toward the Danes' harsh rule from 1016 to 1042, the workmen angrily kicked at the skull, moving it back and forth across the field. A group of boys watching the workers also dug up a skull and began kicking it. They made a game of it and called it "Kicking the Dane's Head." But there was one problem: many boys played without shoes, and the skull hurt their feet. So one day a boy showed up with an inflated cow bladder, which was much easier on the feet and could be kicked farther.

The sport became popular, and towns formed teams to challenge other nearby towns. But in 1189, when King Henry II discovered his subjects spending more time kicking a cow's bladder than practicing their archery, he banned what had become known as "futeball." The game remained outlawed in England for 400 years. When it resumed, it became what we know as soccer.

Walter Camp is credited with creating American football. A student at Yale, he played in the first Yale-Harvard game in 1875. Camp invented the line of scrimmage for starting plays, and the first scoring system. He began the practice of selecting All-American teams, and headed the sport's rules committee for 25 years.

The Irish created a similar but rougher game in the 16th century called Gaelic football (renamed rugby by William Ellis of Rugby College in 1823). Unlike soccer, which did not allow players to use their hands or pick up the ball, rugby players could run with the ball.

American football grew out of a dispute over soccer rules, with an assist from rugby. On November 6, 1869, Princeton and Rutgers played the first college soccer game. At Harvard University in the spring of 1871, a group of students formed a team and modified the game, calling it the "Boston Game," which allowed players to pick up the ball and run with it, as in rugby.

Harvard's players believed their game was so superior they refused to attend a convention in 1873 to draft rules for collegiate soccer matches. As a result, they had to find other competition. On May 15, 1874, Harvard played McGill University of Montreal under the Boston rules of "rugby football." The ball was egg-shaped instead of round, and the emphasis was more on running with the ball than kicking it. If a ball carrier was tackled and he did not toss the ball to a teammate, or the ball went out of bounds, a "scrum" occurred. The ball was placed between the two teams and the linemen fought for possession. Four of McGill's 15 players could not make the trip, so each side played with 11 instead of 15.

American football as we know it today began to take shape in 1880, when the Yale rugby captain, Walter Camp, became disenchanted with the disorderly way in which rugby was played. He created the line of scrimmage (a term from scrummage in rugby), with the two teams

facing each other and one team controlling the ball. But there was no limit to how long a team could have possession, keeping the ball until they scored or punted or fumbled. That made for dull games. In 1881, Yale and Princeton played a scoreless game before 10,000 bored spectators in New York. Princeton held the ball most of the first half, and Yale did the same for the entire second half.

Acting on a writer's suggestion, Camp changed the rules to require a team to gain five yards or lose 10 in three downs to keep the ball. This created the gridiron effect of fields marked with chalk lines every five yards.

Camp did not like the rugby scoring system, in which a touchdown simply gave a team an opportunity for a free kick field goal and a

Rugby, a forerunner of football and a rougher game, combines aspects of soccer, hockey, basketball, and football. Still a popular game in Great Britain, where it evolved from soccer, rugby was popular in America by 1874. It was soon transformed into football, but Americans won the rugby championship of the Olympic Games in 1920 and 1924.

safety yielded no points. Camp believed that a touchdown should count for something and that a team should be rewarded for tackling a ball carrier in his own end zone. In 1883 he created a new scoring system: one point for a safety, two for a touchdown, four for a kicked goal following a touchdown, and five for a field goal. By 1912, changes brought the value of a touchdown up to six points, with a one-point conversion and three points for a field goal.

Camp also created the offensive lineup of seven linemen, a quarterback, two halfbacks, and a fullback. He invented game plans and quarterbacks' signals. But he considered the game his baby and resisted many other rule changes. He opposed huddles and insisted that linemen stand straight up instead of

Before the forward pass was legal, the "flying wedge" was a devastating formation spearheading the running attack. The entire team formed a v-shaped juggernaut in front of the ball carrier and mowed down the defense.

crouching. He did not like throwing the ball, and he added rules restricting quarterbacks' movements and how far they could throw a pass. If a pass was incomplete, the opposing team got the ball. In 1906, other coaches over-ruled Camp and opened up the passing game. The yardage required for a first down was changed from five to 10, and the rule of allowing a team to keep the ball if they lost 10 yards was abolished.

Over the years many rules changed: the field was reduced from 110 to 100 yards in 1912; helmets became mandatory; goal posts were moved from the goal line back 10 yards. But the most significant change happened because of World War II.

Prior to 1943, football players were known as "60-Minute Men" because they played offense and defense. Substitutes were limited by the rules. But when the war put many young players into the military service, veteran players too old to be drafted replaced them. They could no longer go 60 minutes on the field. So the NFL changed the rules to allow substitutes to come and go freely.

Free substitution was never intended to be a permanent part of the game. Nobody had a clue that it would lead to special teams, pass rushers, run defenders, and kicking specialists. In 1946, a year after the war ended, free substitution was reduced to just three replacements at a time, but three years later the NFL went back to open substitution and the modern age of football in America began.

3

THE PIONEERS

As Walter Camp's version of football spread throughout Northeastern colleges, it also reached many city athletic associations, which were the greatest source of spectator sports for most communities. Fans flocked to the games, creating the neighborhood spirit toward football in the fall that baseball enjoyed in the spring and summer.

College players could lose their eligibility if they accepted money to play, and the athletic associations were governed by a national union that could punish them for paying players. Still, some of the best college players were paid, and they played under false names.

Football's first professionals evolved from a battle between two Pittsburgh teams, the Allegheny Athletic Association and the Pittsburgh Athletic Club. Neither team was happy about the result of a hotly contested 6–6 tie on October 21, 1892. As they worked toward a rematch on November 12, both teams quietly recruited outstanding college players.

They both went after three-time All-American guard Pudge Heffelfinger of Yale, who secretly accepted $500 and $25 expenses from Allegheny, to the dismay of the Pittsburgh club. Amid claims and counterclaims of professionalism that forced the cancellation of all bets on the game, Allegheny won, 4–0, on a snowy day when Heffelfinger forced a fumble, picked up the ball, and raced 25 yards for the score. The payment

After three years as an All-American halfback at Illinois, Red Grange drew record crowds on an exhibition game tour with the Chicago Bears in the winter of 1925–1926. Known as the "Galloping Ghost" for his elusive running, Grange was also a defensive star for the Bears.

to Heffelfinger remained a secret for 70 years, until old account books of the team were discovered.

The first openly professional player was John Brallier, a high school quarterback in Latrobe, Pennsylvania. The local YMCA team paid him $10 to play for them in 1895. When Latrobe played nearby rival Jeannette later that year, every player received $10 in the first all-professional game.

Professional football spread throughout the Midwest. Most players were hired per game and paid from the gate receipts. Players switched teams from week to week. The games were marred by frequent fights and heavy gambling. In 1906, the Canton, Ohio, Bulldogs hired four players from arch-rival Massillon. When Massillon won the game, accusations of throwing the game killed football in Canton until 1911, when a young man named Jack Cusack became the team's manager.

Cusack, who was later instrumental in bringing the Pro Football Hall of Fame to Canton, sparked national attention for the game in 1915 when he signed Olympic track star Jim Thorpe for $250 a game. Thorpe's presence boosted Canton attendance from 1,200 a game to about 8,000. Soon more former college players began to sign with pro teams, including Notre Dame coach Knute Rockne, who coached his team on Saturday and played on Sunday for whichever team paid him the most.

In 1919, Curly Lambeau, an employee of the Indian Packing Co. in Green Bay, Wisconsin, went to his boss and asked him to sponsor a football team. The boss agreed, and Lambeau called his team the Packers. But bad weather and poor attendance hurt the team. By 1922,

they were broke. Football fans in the small town in Wisconsin rescued the Packers by buying shares of stock at $5. The Packers threw in a season ticket as part of the deal. Green Bay remains the smallest city in major league sports, with a population under 100,000.

Seeking some form of organization, the leaders of 10 pro teams met on September 17, 1920, at Hay's Hupmobile Showroom in Canton. They formed the American Professional Football Association and named Jim Thorpe president. Except for Detroit and Chicago, the teams were in small towns. They added another team to start the season, and three more joined along the way. The first game took place September 26, 1920, with the Rock Island, Illinois, Independents beating the St. Paul, Minnesota, Ideals, 48–0. Akron, with a 6–0–3 record, won a four-team playoff for the first professional championship.

On August 31, 1895, the Latrobe, Pa., YMCA fielded the first all-professional team against the rival Jeannette Athletic Club. John Brallier, the first openly professional football player, is in the front row, third from the right.

Jim Thorpe was America's greatest athlete. Born in Oklahoma of French, Irish, and Native American ancestry, Thorpe starred for the Canton Bulldogs in the pre-NFL days of 1915–1919. He also played baseball with the New York Giants during those years and won both the pentathlon and decathlon in the 1912 Olympics.

But the league was ineffective. Each team made its own schedule; there were no formal standings or required number of games. The next year Joe Carr replaced Thorpe as president and brought the game the direction it needed. He renamed the association the National Football League. He moved teams out of small towns into bigger cities, including George Halas's Decatur Staleys, who moved to Chicago. Hoping to ride on the popularity of the baseball Cubs, Halas named his team the Bears. In 1925, Tim Mara paid $500 for the New York franchise that he called the Giants after the popular baseball team.

The Canton Bulldogs dominated the league's early years, going undefeated in 24 games in 1922 and 1923. In 1923, they outscored opponents 246–19, led by tailback Lou Smythe, the only player to lead the league in passing and rushing touchdowns in one year. But the Bulldogs, like most of the smaller teams, struggled to make a profit and moved to Cleveland in 1924.

As often happens in any business, the new league spawned competition. After the 1925 season, Red Grange, a much-publicized running back from Illinois, played in an exhibition tour with the Chicago Bears. Grange drew huge crowds wherever they played, and he earned $100,000 for himself from the tour. When he refused the Bears' offer for 1926, his agent put together a new, nine-team league, the American Football League, and Grange signed with the New York Yankees squad.

By taking in just about every town that wanted a franchise in 1926, the National League swelled to 23 teams, but more than half of them disappeared by 1927.

With two teams in major cities fighting for fans and attention, the season was a disaster for everybody. With the exception of games in which Grange played, the AFL barely drew enough fans to open the hot dog stands. Teams dropped out almost every week; by the end of the season, only four remained. The next year, 12 of the 23 NFL teams folded. Only 83 paying fans witnessed a Giants-Bears game in New York.

One reason for pro football's lack of success was the game itself. From 1920 to 1932, almost two-thirds of the games were shutouts. Strategy emphasized defense and field position. Teams often punted on third down to pin their opponents deep in their own territory. The rules discouraged passing and scoring. A pass had to be thrown from at least five yards behind the line of scrimmage. If a team threw an incompletion in the end zone, they lost possession of the ball. In 1927, even field goals were made harder when owners moved the goal posts to the back of the end zone.

Realizing the need for changes, the league gradually opened up the offense. George Halas, one of the league's founders and owner/coach of the Chicago Bears, emerged as the most influential leader. For more than 60 years, Papa Bear ran the Bears and, some said, the league. A rule change rarely passed without his approval. Halas was a great visionary who understood the value of star players, marketing, and making the game entertaining. He built championship teams in the 1930s and '40s around a powerful running game and bone-crushing defense. But it was the passing game that would lift professional football to a new level of success.

4

SLINGIN' INTO THE SPOTLIGHT

The 1936 NFL Championship between the Green Bay Packers and Boston Redskins was played in New York because no one in Boston gave a bean about the Redskins. It was the first time prior to the beginning of the Super Bowl in 1967 that the title game was played at a neutral site, and it helped set in motion a series of events that would change the NFL forever.

Redskins owner George Preston Marshall had lost $90,000 on the team in five years. To attract fans, he once hired a full-blooded Indian to coach the team. Another time he ordered his players to wear war paint on their faces. The Redskins were also the first to parade a marching band at halftime. Nothing helped, not even winning. When only 11,220 fans showed up for a late-season game against the Packers in 1936, Marshall openly hunted for a new home.

Three days after the Packers won the championship, 21–6, in New York, Marshall announced that he was moving his team to Washington. Marshall was a shrewd businessman who understood the value of having a star player to promote. His Redskins had future Hall of Famers in running back Cliff Battles, receiver Wayne Milner, and tackle Turk Edwards. But he needed something more spectacular.

During business trips to Texas he had read about a quarterback for Texas Christian University named Slingin' Sammy Baugh. In an

Slingin' Sammy Baugh was a famous passer for the Washington Redskins in the 1930s and '40s. But he was also a six-time All-Pro as a punter, runner, and defensive back. Baugh led the Redskins to two championships and to the finals four other times. He put many passing and punting records in the books during his 16-year career.

era when teams rarely passed more than 10 times a game, Baugh was lighting up the Southwestern skies like fireworks. Slingin' Sam would not hesitate to throw long on first down and pass 20 to 25 times a game. Baugh was not only an accurate passer but an excellent punter as well. As a boy he had practiced throwing footballs through a tire swinging from a tree. Then he would place a rag 50 yards down the field and practice kicking right to the spot.

Neither college nor professional football had ever seen anything like Baugh. When Marshall saw crowds of up to 80,000 watching Baugh play for TCU in 1936, he knew he had found the star attraction he needed. The Redskins drafted Baugh with the eighth pick in the first round and made him the highest-paid player in football at $7,000.

Baugh's impact was immediate. In his first game for the Redskins, he completed 11 of 16 passes for 116 yards in a 13–3 victory against the Giants. His five incompletions were dropped passes. Washington was electrified and so were football fans everywhere. Stadiums throughout the NFL sold out to see the brilliant passer, who led the Redskins to the 1937 championship.

The NFL had rarely been blessed with a star of such humility, ability, and drawing power. With his dry, Texas wit and easygoing nature, Baugh was popular with teammates, fans, media, and even opponents. He often stayed hours after games signing autographs on the field, and he spent much of his free time making public appearances or giving clinics on passing.

Baugh's arrival coincided with the pro game's efforts to break away from its run-and-defense mode. "They thought they wanted a running game and a defensive game," Baugh said. "Every rule was against making you want to throw the ball. I thought it was a very conservative game. But after my first year, more teams started passing the ball. They finally realized that people like to see scoring. You don't want to sit out there in the cold and see a 14–6 game."

Because of Baugh, Marshall and George Halas supported changes in the rules to increase the passer's protection. "The linemen could hit you after the whistle blew," Baugh said. "It was the silliest rule you ever saw. Sometimes those linemen would chase the quarterback 20 yards and the ball would be 70 yards away with the guy running with it. Mr. Marshall asked me if I thought it would help the passing game if they came up with a rule that said the quarterback couldn't be hit after the play was blown dead. I said, 'Sure, it'll add a few years to his life.'"

Baugh became football's most visible star, his popularity equal to Joe DiMaggio and Ted Williams in baseball, Jesse Owens in track, and Joe Louis in boxing. He inspired a generation of youngsters to become passers, and he opened the eyes of coaches, who began to look for new ways to make passing part of their game plan.

By the time Baugh retired in 1952, he had won two NFL titles and five division championships with the Redskins. He led the league in passing six times and punting four times. His 45.1 yards per kick career punting average and 51.3 yards per kick for the 1940 season are still NFL records.

But Sammy Baugh did not have the most outstanding pass receiver in the league. In Green Bay, the Packers had signed Don Hutson from the University of Alabama in 1935 to team with the first of the long passers, Arnie Herber. The Herber-to-Hutson combination ran up more completions and touchdowns than any other passing attack in the game. Hutson ran 100 yards in 9.7 seconds, causing George Halas to say, "I just concede him two touchdowns a game and hope we can score."

Hutson's first NFL catch was good for 83 yards. In 11 years he caught 488 passes, 99 for touchdowns. He also loved to kick. In a 1944 game against Detroit, he caught four TD passes and kicked five extra points for 29 points in a single quarter, a record that still stands. He led the Packers to three championships and four Western Division titles. By the time he retired in 1945, Hutson held almost every receiving record.

The running game had its early stars, too. The Bears, who won championships in 1933, '40, '41, '43, and '46, had a bruising runner in Bronko Nagurski. Nagurski inspired legends like Paul Bunyan did—tall tales that couldn't possibly be true. But most of the Nagurski stories were true. At 6' 2" and 230 pounds, he was so strong, said one story, that a University of Minnesota coach discovered him plowing a field without a horse. During one game, Nagurski barreled through the end zone with such force that he knocked over a mounted policeman and his horse. On a touchdown run against the Redskins, he knocked two linebackers in opposite directions, bowled over a defensive back, and flattened a safety before careening off the goal posts and stumbling into the stadium's brick wall.

When the Bears refused to pay him $6,000 in 1938, Nagurski became a professional wrestler. He returned to the Bears in 1943, helped them win another title, then retired again.

By the time Nagurski departed for good, the Bears had their own star quarterback in Sid Luckman of Columbia University. He and Baugh waged epic battles for years. But the most famous of their encounters ended in

It was said of Bronko Nagurski (seen here carrying the ball) that he was "the only man who ever lived who could lead his own interference." An All-American fullback and tackle at Minnesota, Nagurski was a 60-minute strongman for the Chicago Bears 1930–1938, then became a pro wrestler. Said one coach, "There's only one defense that would stop Nagurski— shoot him before he leaves the dressing room."

As a rookie with the Chicago Bears in 1940, Duke All-American George McAfee ran back a kickoff 93 yards in his first game. Here he scores in the Bears' 73–0 rout of the Washington Redskins in the 1940 NFL championship game.

the most one-sided NFL championship game in history.

The week before the Bears and Redskins squared off for the 1940 title, Washington owner George Preston Marshall made the mistake of calling the Bears a bunch of crybabies, sore losers, and quitters. The Bears were so mad at Marshall they went out and buried the favored Redskins, 73–0. The Bears scored so often they ran out of footballs and finished the game with an old practice ball and orders from the officials not to kick any more extra points. "The touchdowns came so quickly there for a while," said announcer Red Barber, "I felt like I was the cashier at a grocery."

The Bears featured the T-formation, which spread out the offense and placed the quarterback in a better position to pass. In 12 seasons Luckman led the Bears to four NFL titles and was All-Pro five times. A native of Brooklyn, his greatest day came in 1943 in New York on "Sid Luckman Day." He threw for a record 443 yards and seven touchdowns.

On that same day, Sammy Baugh enjoyed the greatest individual game in the history of the NFL. Against Detroit, he passed for four touchdowns, intercepted four passes, and averaged 52 yards a punt. He and Luckman tied for passing honors that year and once again faced each other in the title game. The Bears won that one, too.

The pass-happy offense made popular by Baugh and Luckman and, later, Otto Graham, led more teams to install the T-formation in place of the traditional single wing used by teams such as the Redskins. By 1946 only the Steelers clung to the old-style attack.

World War II almost shut down the NFL as about 360 players and front office employees went into the armed forces. The Philadelphia Eagles and Pittsburgh Steelers combined their teams. Sammy Baugh, Sid Luckman, and Don Hutson were exempt from military duty, and their play helped keep the NFL in business and boosted the morale of the country every Sunday in the fall. Most of all, their accomplishments built the foundation for all the players, and the game of football, that would follow them.

5 POSTWAR BOOM

In 1946, the first year after World War II ended, pro football expanded. Taking advantage of a national prosperity, a group of wealthy owners started the All-American Football Conference, with the Los Angeles Dons and San Francisco 49ers bringing the game to the West Coast for the first time. The NFL allowed the champion Cleveland Rams to move to Los Angeles to compete with the new league, and the AAFC put a team in Cleveland, which was named after its coach, Paul Brown.

Brown and the AAFC revolutionized the pro game. The Browns signed running back Marion Motley and guard Bill Willis, the first African-American players in the league since 1933. The Rams signed black stars Kenny Washington, the 1939 college rushing champion at UCLA, and Woody Strode. Before long every team—except the Washington Redskins, who held out until 1962—had African-American players.

Paul Brown was the first pro coach to hire full-time assistants. He gave players intelligence tests to judge their ability to learn his complex system, and he introduced playbooks and classroom game instruction. He was the first to test the 40-yard speed of players and to use game films to grade his men. He began the use of substitute players who would take in plays to the quarterback.

Broadway Joe Namath, pro football's most colorful personality from 1966 to 1977, made headlines when he boldly guaranteed that his underdog New York Jets would defeat the Baltimore Colts in Super Bowl III in 1969. Here Namath (12) gets a pass away despite heavy pressure from the Colts in the Jets' 16–7 upset.

The Browns won all four AAFC championships behind quarterback Otto Graham before the league folded after the 1949 season. The Browns, 49ers, and Baltimore Colts then joined the NFL. The Browns continued to dominate, winning NFL titles in 1950, '54, and '55.

Despite the faster-paced, higher-scoring games and the electrifying new stars, most pro teams were losing money. The competition for players between the two leagues had sent salaries soaring, eating up all the gains in attendance. The AAFC's demise left the NFL with 13 teams. But stability was still out of reach. The Baltimore Colts folded after 1950, and the New York Yankees moved to Dallas in 1952, then to Baltimore a year later.

NFL commissioner Bert Bell looked at the new television industry as a possible source of revenue for football. By the mid-1950s, most teams televised their road games back home, and the networks carried some games. Although this exposure helped the game's popularity and attendance to grow locally, the earning potential remained untapped. The dramatic, nationally televised 1958 Colts-Giants championship opened the way to a new prosperity.

Watching that famous game helped to convince oil millionaire Lamar Hunt to pursue an NFL team for Dallas. But the league rejected him. That didn't stop Hunt. He started a new league, the American Football League, with teams in Boston, Buffalo, Los Angeles, New York, Dallas, Denver, and Houston. When ABC television agreed to pay the AFL to televise games for five years, the league's survival was guaranteed, and the partnership between football and television was born.

Another salary war began as the AFL and NFL competed head-to-head for players and publicity. The war between the leagues often overshadowed the play on the field. In the summer of 1966, NFL commissioner Pete Rozelle concluded a peace treaty, leading eventually to a merger of the two leagues. The first dividend of the peace was the start of the AFL-NFL Championship game in 1967.

The fan appeal for the World Series of football started slowly. Vince Lombardi's Green Bay

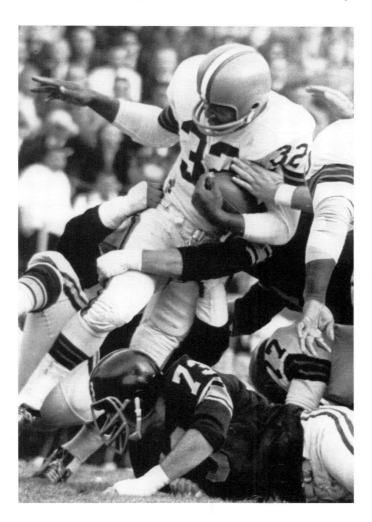

It took three or four Pittsburgh Steelers to stop the Cleveland Browns' Jim Brown in this 1963 game. An outstanding five-sport star, Brown won many votes as pro football's all-time greatest running back in his nine years with the Browns.

Packers, led by quarterback Bart Starr, had dominated the NFL in the 1960s, winning five championships in seven years. When they defeated the AFL's Kansas City Chiefs in the first AFL-NFL Championship at the Los Angeles Coliseum, the game fell 30,000 short of a sellout. It wasn't until 1969, after the Packers had repeated as champions, that the event became known as the Super Bowl. When the New York Jets, led by their flashy quarterback, Broadway Joe Namath, upset the heavily favored Baltimore Colts in Super Bowl III, the event was on its way to becoming the most-watched television event every year.

With the merger of the two leagues completed in 1970, ABC launched "Monday Night Football," which brought unprecedented money and exposure to the game. By 1978, a poll showed that 70 percent of the nation's sports fans said they followed pro football, compared to 54 percent who followed baseball.

Prosperity came with a troublesome price. The players went on strike during the exhibition season in 1974 and again just before the 1975 season. No games were canceled, but the players were making it clear they deserved a bigger share of the television revenues and increased ticket sales. Prosperity also attracted another would-be competitor. The World Football League opened in 1974 with 12 teams, half of them in NFL cities. They lured some top-flight players, but the league lasted less than two years, leaving $30 million in debts in its wake.

The NFL experienced constant turmoil in the 1980s. The Oakland Raiders sued for the right to move to Los Angeles, and they succeeded in 1982. The Baltimore Colts loaded their equipment into a moving van in the middle of the night and sped away to Indianapolis in 1984. The St. Louis Cardinals switched to Phoenix in 1987.

The restless players went on strike for 57 days in 1982, resulting in the first October with no pro football since 1919. (In 1987, the players would walk out again, this time for 24 days, but the league would continue play by using replacement players.) And in 1983, another rival appeared—the 12-team United States Football League. The new league avoided direct competition with the NFL by playing in the spring and summer. It succeeded in signing some college stars, such as Heisman Trophy winners Doug Flutie, Mike Rozier, and Herschel Walker, and future NFL stars Reggie White, Steve Young, and Jim Kelly. Once again the competition for players boosted salaries.

Then the USFL made a mistake. In 1986, it decided to switch to a fall schedule and challenge the NFL. When the USFL failed to get a TV contract, it was forced to go out of business. The USFL owners sued the NFL for blocking their TV bid and won a hollow victory; the court awarded them all of $3, not enough to cover their $150 million in debts.

Despite its growing pains and the toll of fighting off competitors and satisfying its players, the NFL remained prosperous through its policy of sharing all national television revenues among its teams—and by introducing a steady parade of new stars to captivate its growing legion of fans.

6 STAR POWER

Sammy Baugh's passing led to the brilliance of Otto Graham, Johnny Unitas, Joe Namath, Joe Montana, and Dan Marino.

Don Hutson's speed and receiving skills led to Lionel Taylor, Fred Biletnikoff, James Lofton, and Jerry Rice.

Beattie Feathers' running led to Steve Van Buren, Jim Brown, O. J. Simpson, Eric Dickerson, and Emmitt Smith.

And George Halas's coaching led to Paul Brown, Vince Lombardi, Don Shula, and Bill Walsh.

Players became progressively better over the years, and statistics demonstrate that no era had more efficient passers, prolific runners, or better receivers than the late 20th century.

It all began with Johnny Unitas, who led the Baltimore Colts to three championships and one Super Bowl victory. "The thing about Unitas," said Sammy Baugh, "is he may have been the best of all. He did everything. He could pass and he could direct. He knew how to call a game and that's what was most impressive about him. He could take control of a game like no one I'd ever seen."

Unitas was a scrawny high school player rejected by every college. The University of Louisville allowed him to play as a walk-on. Later, the Pittsburgh Steelers gave him a tryout but cut him in his first training camp. He was

New York Giants linebacker Lawrence Taylor wraps a forearm around Earnest Byner's head to bring down the Washington running back. The 6' 3", 240-pound Taylor used his size and speed to become the NFL's most intimidating pass rusher and tackler from 1981 to 1993.

working as a pile driver and playing semipro ball on the weekends when the Baltimore Colts signed him for the cost of a long distance phone call.

By the time Unitas retired, he had amassed 40,239 passing yards, 290 TDs, and a seemingly unbreakable streak of 47 consecutive games in which he passed for a score. He will always be best remembered for his cool approach to the final minutes of the 1958 championship game, which the unflappable Unitas later referred to as "really just another football game as far as I'm concerned."

Six years later the upstart American Football League's New York Jets signed Joe Namath out of the University of Alabama for a whopping $400,000, gaining the new league huge headlines and instant credibility. The NFL was stunned. The handsome, flamboyant quarterback attracted fans of all ages and both sexes. Television commercials made Namath the most recognized player.

But Namath was more than glamour and hype. He had a brilliant arm but fragile knees. From 1970 to 1973 he missed 28 of 50 games with injuries. When he was healthy, few were better. In 1967 he passed for a record 4,007 yards. One week he threw six interceptions in a half; the next week he completed 15 straight passes. Three times he threw for more than 400 yards.

Like Unitas, Namath is remembered most for one game. Prior to Super Bowl III in 1969, Namath told a gathering that his underdog Jets would defeat the 17-point favorite Baltimore Colts. "I guarantee it," he said. When he delivered on his promise in a 16–7 upset, he ran off

Known as "Joe Cool," quarterback Joe Montana's reputation for last-minute victories and come-from-behind heroics began at Notre Dame and continued with the San Francisco 49ers, where he became the first three-time Super Bowl MVP.

the field holding his right index finger high in the air.

Joe Montana had a similar trademark gesture. After a touchdown, he would throw his arms in the air as if helping the official to make the call. That was as expressive as the quiet, unassuming Joe Cool ever got. "He'd get in that huddle and get a look in his eye," said Sam Wyche, who coached the rookie quarterback for the San Francisco 49ers in 1979. "He was saying, 'This is a lock. This is going to work.'"

From high school through his years at Notre Dame and into the pros, Montana led 34 come-from-behind victories. Some of them are legendary. With 51 seconds to play in the 1981 NFC title game against Dallas, he found Dwight Clark in the back of the end zone for "The Catch" and a 28–27 win. After missing nine weeks in 1986 following spinal disk surgery, his career appeared to be over. But he returned against Washington and set career highs with 60 passes and 441 yards.

In 1989, the 49ers trailed by three points in Super Bowl XXIII. They had the ball on their 8-yard line with 3 minutes, 20 seconds to play. Montana walked into the huddle and looked into the peering, nervous eyes of his teammates. Suddenly he pointed into the first few rows of Miami's Joe Robbie Stadium and exclaimed, "Hey! That's [actor] John Candy over there." That broke the tension. Montana then directed "The Drive," completing seven of eight passes, the last a 10-yard scoring strike to John Taylor with 34 seconds remaining, to beat the Cincinnati Bengals, 20–16.

Montana's numbers say he may have been the greatest quarterback of all time: four Super Bowl victories without a single interception; three times NFL MVP; highest career passing rating (93.1) and career completion percentage (63.67); and NFL records for completions, yards, and touchdowns in playoffs.

Those were numbers and Super Bowl records that made Dan Marino of the Miami Dolphins envious. The last quarterback taken in the first round of the 1983 draft, Marino led the Dolphins to the Super Bowl in his rookie year. They lost to Washington, but Marino figured there would be more chances. It never happened.

The Dolphins, who had gone through the entire 1972 season and playoffs undefeated, had poor teams in the late 1980s and early 1990s. They lacked a running game. But Marino kept throwing until he became the career leader in yards, completions, attempts, and touchdowns.

The Dolphins may have had greater success if they had had a running back like Jim Brown. But then, there was only one Jim Brown. At 6' 2" and 232 bruising pounds, Brown ran over, past, and through defenders with ease. He played nine seasons (1957–1965), winning the rushing title eight times. He never carried the ball fewer than 200 times a year, and he never missed a game. Brown ran up 58 100-yard games and was All-Pro in every season he played. He was only 29 when he quit to become an actor. But he left behind career records of 12,312 yards and 236 touchdowns that stood for more than 20 years.

O. J. Simpson broke Brown's single-season rushing record of 1,863 in 1973. Needing just 60 yards in the Buffalo Bills' final game, Simpson easily passed Brown's mark by rolling up 108 yards in the first half. Suddenly another goal was within reach.

"At the end of the third quarter, Joe Ferguson, our quarterback, came down to the bench to where the offense was," Simpson recalled. "He said, 'Juice only needs 50 yards for 2,000. Let's get it.'"

Simpson finished the day with 2,003 yards—a total deemed virtually out of reach. Ten years later another speedster, Eric

Dickerson of the Rams, came along and broke Simpson's record by rushing for 2,105 yards in 1984.

But for endurance and consistency, the Chicago Bears' Walter Payton stood out as the best of all time. Payton missed only one game in 13 seasons, retiring in 1987 with the most career rushing yards and the single-game record of 275. Just 5' 10" and weighing 202, Payton had no fear of running inside. In eight of his first 10 seasons he averaged more than 20 carries a game. He seemed to get better as he got older, becoming the first back to have three consecutive 1,000-yard seasons in his thirties.

Walter Payton runs through the snowflakes and Giants tacklers with equal ease in a 1977 game. Well-liked for his even disposition, Payton was the NFL's all-time leading rusher when he retired in 1987 after 13 seasons with the Chicago Bears.

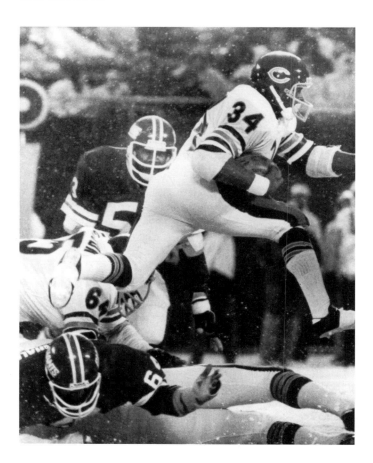

The Cowboys' Emmitt Smith was to the 1990s what Payton was to the '80s. Quick, elusive, and durable, Smith set the pace for Dallas. He rolled up 1,484 yards en route to a Super Bowl victory in 1994 and gained 1,773 yards on the way to the Cowboys' 1996 championship.

As the 20th century came to a close, the Detroit Lions' Barry Sanders was running right into the record books. In 1997 he became the first player both to rush for 1500 yards in four consecutive years and to rush for 1000 yards in nine straight seasons.

The San Francisco 49ers' Jerry Rice knew about piling up yardage, topping all the great receivers in history when it came to catching passes and gaining yards. Working with Joe Montana, Rice became a game-breaker. He often left his pass routes and waved to Montana, who would invariably find him wide open. It took Rice just eight seasons to pass Don Hutson's 99 career touchdowns, a record that had stood for 44 years.

Rice took so much pride in his ability to get free in double- and triple-team coverages that quarterback Steve Young, Montana's successor, said, "I think he believes that if they covered him with 11 guys, he should still be open and win the game."

Not all the game's stars were on offense. Some defensive players had enough impact to change the game. Defensive tackle Mean Joe Greene was the cornerstone of the Steelers' "Steel Curtain" defense that helped them win four Super Bowls in the the 1970s. Linebacker Dick Butkus of the Bears was so fierce that he said, "When I hit a guy, I wanted him to know who hit him without his ever having to look around and check the number."

San Francisco safety Ronnie Lott hit so hard and was so expert at reading passes that offenses avoided him. When finger surgery threatened to sideline him for a few games, Lott had the fingertip amputated instead. And no defensive end was better than Green Bay's Reggie White, an ordained Baptist minister whose ability to sack quarterbacks was outdone only by his willingness to help other people off the field.

But two defensive players changed football in the late 20th century: linebacker Lawrence Taylor and cornerback Deion Sanders. Taylor led the New York Giants to Super Bowl wins in 1986 and 1990, and he played in a record 10 Pro Bowls. Taylor was a ferocious and virtually unstoppable pass rusher, forcing teams to design their game plans around him. For 13 seasons he was "like a cop putting sirens on his car," said a teammate. Taylor made linebacking the cool position, and a generation of kids copied his renegade style and wore his number 56.

Sanders, with his gold chains and nicknames of "Neon" and "Prime Time," became football's most flamboyant star since Joe Namath. But it was no act. Sanders was so quick that teams simply avoided passing to his side of the field. He helped the 49ers and Cowboys to Super Bowl wins and played major league baseball between football seasons, becoming the first to appear in a World Series and the Super Bowl.

Not all of pro football's stars were players. Coach Bill Walsh of the 49ers was one of the best at judging talent. A brilliant offensive tactician, Walsh built the 49ers into the team of the '80s. He selected Joe Montana in the third round of the draft because of Joe's character, not his arm. He took Jerry Rice, an unknown receiver at Mississippi Valley State, because of his instincts and speed. Walsh had coached under the strict organizational hand of Paul Brown, and he made his teams understand that high expectations would lead to success. From 1981 to '89, the 49ers grasped the lesson: they had the best regular season records and won three Super Bowls. But Walsh was just as proud of his assistants who became head coaches; six had NFL jobs in 1995, and one of them, Mike Holmgren, coached the 1997 Super Bowl champion Green Bay Packers.

Like Paul Brown in Cleveland, Vince Lombardi created an early dynasty in Green Bay. Strict and demanding, Lombardi was a master at motivating a team. His players respected him and his authority. "When he says, 'Sit down,' I don't even bother to look for a chair," a Packer player once said. Lombardi taught his players how to be winners on and off the field. In his nine seasons beginning in 1959, they won six division titles and five championships. Lombardi died of stomach cancer in 1970. The trophy awarded to the Super Bowl winner is named for him.

When the Dolphins' Don Shula retired in 1996, he was the all-time winningest coach, with 347 victories in 33 years. Shula won two Super Bowls and reached the title game four other times. His 1972 Dolphins, who were 17–0, were the only team to go through the regular season and postseason without a loss or tie.

GAUGES OF GREATNESS

Unlike baseball, which has milestones such as 300 victories for a pitcher or 3,000 hits for a batter, football uses a different measure for greatness. Rushing and passing yards, touchdowns, tackles, and other statistics are important. But the era in which a player performed and the rules and style of the game at that time make statistical records less reliable in comparing football stars. All-Pro selections, championships, and longevity are often more indicative of a football player's level of performance.

"When you say Joe Montana threw for 400 yards in a game, that's great, but if Joe Namath threw for 300 that might be more impressive, because of the difference in eras and rules," said Hall of Fame curator Joe Horrigan. "That's why you're always reluctant to say one player is the best of all time. You have to judge them on their era. Rules changes have historically made a huge impact, and 20 years can be a big difference in an era."

"The sport is subjective," said football historian Bob Carroll. "Some positions, such as linemen, are not measurable by stats, and that leaves it open to intangibles. But other positions have standard issues: was the quarterback a great passer or a great leader? Bob Griese was a great leader, but Dan Marino was a great passer. Griese brought intangibles, Marino brought great tools, like Bobby Layne did."

Teaming with Joe Montana, Jerry Rice of the 49ers combined sticky fingers with swift and shifty open-field running to rack up records for wide receivers. Here he hangs onto a pass while Miami's Troy Vincent hangs onto him in a 1991 game.

Quarterbacks benefited from modern rules that restricted the defense and gave them better protection. Offensive players counter that the rules changes simply leveled the playing field. "Athletes on defense are so good and so strong now that you can't beat them 11 on 11," said 49ers quarterback Steve Young.

Statistics can be misleading. Records are an inadequate measure of greatness. One example is the method of computing quarterback ratings by a formula combining average yards per pass attempt, touchdown and interception percentages per attempt, and completion percentage. In the 1990s, NFL offenses shifted from a power game to finesse and speed. As a result, quarterbacks who were short passers and rarely went for the big play, such as Dave Krieg, had a higher QB rating than Hall of Famer Terry Bradshaw, a renowned bomber who won four Super Bowls with the Pittsburgh Steelers. Krieg's 81.9 rating ranked him number 11, compared to Bradshaw's 70.9, which put him at number 71.

A 1,000-yard-rushing or 100-reception season was no longer considered spectacular. In 1995 alone, a record-tying 16 rushers passed 1,000 yards, and 23 receivers gained at least 1,000. The lengthening of the season from 14 to 16 games in 1978 meant a rusher could average under 63 yards a game and still reach 1,000.

None of this proved that the running game was actually better than in the past. From 1986 to 1996, only 10 players averaged more than five yards per carry in reaching 1,000. Jim Brown accomplished that five times.

In 1990, Jerry Rice, widely considered the greatest receiver in history, became the fourth to catch at least 100 passes in a season. It was considered a terrific milestone. But in the next six years, 19 other players had at least 100 catches.

Still, some incredible feats remain in the record books, some that will never be matched and are worth remembering:

From 1956 to 1960, Johnny Unitas threw at least one touchdown pass in 47 consecutive games.

From 1946 to 1955, Otto Graham led the Cleveland Browns to the championship every year, the equivalent of reaching the Super Bowl 10 consecutive years.

On Thanksgiving Day 1929, Ernie Nevers scored all 40 of the Chicago Cardinals' points with six rushing touchdowns and four extra points against the Chicago Bears. His is the oldest NFL record in the books. (Nevers was also a big-league pitcher for three years with the St. Louis Browns.)

Most passing records have a short life, but the Rams' Norm Van Brocklin set one on September 21, 1951, that may never be touched. Against the New York Yankees, he completed 27 of 41 passes for five touchdowns and 554 yards in a 54–14 victory.

Sammy Baugh of the Redskins averaged a phenomenal 51.4 yards per punt in 1940, and in 1943 he became the only player ever to lead the league in passing, punting, and interceptions.

Cleveland Browns running back Jim Brown played nine seasons and won eight rushing titles. He averaged 1,368 yards per season.

In 1984, Eric Dickerson of the Rams set a single-season record with 2,105 yards in 16 games.

Green Bay Packers quarterback Bart Starr threw 294 passes without an interception in 1964–1965.

The Minnesota Vikings' durable defensive end, Jim Marshall, played in 282 consecutive games from 1961 to 1979.

Other records are not out of reach.

Walter Payton set a single-game mark of 275 yards against Minnesota in 1977. Modern defenses are so concerned about the passing game that a Barry Sanders, Curtis Martin, or Emmitt Smith could rush to greater glory.

In 26 seasons, George Blanda accounted for 2,002 points as a quarterback and kicker, but the emphasis on field goals in the late 1990s made it possible that this record could fall.

In 1984, Dan Marino passed for 48 touchdowns and 5,084 yards. Brett Favre and Drew Bledsoe each got within 500 yards, but topping 48 TDs may be more difficult.

Sometimes quarterbacks taste glory; sometimes they eat dirt. Dan Marino once had 759 straight pass attempts without being sacked. Joe Namath was never that lucky.

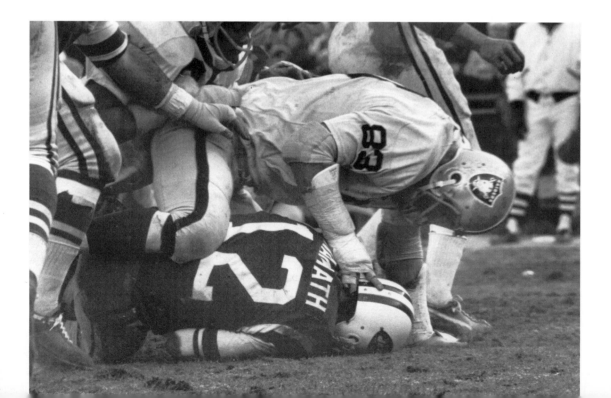

Deacon Jones of the Rams' famous "Fearsome Foursome" defensive line holds the career record for sacks with 172. But Reggie White of Green Bay was closing in by 1998.

In 1970, Tom Dempsey, the Saints' portly kicker, hit a record 63-yard field goal to beat the Detroit Lions. The idea that Dempsey, who had half a foot and wore a special shoe, could make such a kick was so outrageous to Detroit Hall of Famer Alex Karras that Karras laughed at Dempsey when he trotted onto the field. Artificial turf and domed stadiums could make breaking Dempsey's record a possibility.

With so much emphasis on passing, it is hard to believe that two receiving records still stood in 1997: Tom Fears' 18 catches for the Rams against Green Bay in 1950, and the Rams' Flipper Anderson gaining 336 yards against the Saints in 1989.

The Last Time . . .

♦ a player led the NFL in rushes and passes was the Giants' Benny Friedman in 1928.

♦ a game ended in a 0–0 tie was the Giants and Lions in 1943.

♦ a player outscored a team in a season was the Eagles' Steve Van Buren, whose 110 points in 1945 topped the Steelers' 79 and the Cardinals' 98.

♦ a running back had 10 touchdown catches was Johnny Blood in 1931.

♦ a drop-kicked field goal was made was by Dutch Clark in 1937.

♦ a player played without a helmet was the Bears' Dick Plasman in 1941.

♦ a player made All-Pro on offense and defense in his career was Ollie Matson.

♦ the NFL had a winless team was the 0–14 Tampa Bay Buccaneers in 1976.

8 FOOTBALL'S FUTURE

In the early days of professional football, it was difficult to imagine what the future might hold. Few ever dreamed that football would surpass baseball in popularity. In those formative years, no one could have predicted the wide-open passing game, the 1,000-yard rushers, the blitz defenses, and the influence of television.

Since the days of Walter Camp, football has constantly evolved. No major sport adjusted its rules more often. Many of those changes were aimed at improving the safety of the players or maintaining a balance between offense and defense. When the offense found a new formation, like the popular, pass-happy West Coast offense of the mid-1990s, the defense came up with a way to counter it. This created a never-ending chess game of football strategy.

Computer and industrial technologies changed the way players executed plays. Advances in weight training and conditioning continued to make players stronger and faster. Not long ago a 250-pound lineman was considered huge. Soon the average weight might be 300 pounds. Injuries could be a lesser factor as synthetic joints and ligaments make healing faster and easier.

Television continues to affect the game, both its marketing and its planning. Coaches have a video library of plays available at their fingertips just minutes after the play. Fans will be able to watch a game and call for a replay whenever

Brett Favre of the Green Bay Packers gets set to pass against the New England Patriots in the 1997 Super Bowl, won by the Packers, 35–21. The Wisconsin city of 96,000, the smallest to hold a major league sports franchise, celebrated its first championship in 29 years.

Curtis Martin continued the tradition of outstanding running backs that began with Jim Thorpe and Red Grange. Here he scores for the New England Patriots in the 1997 Super Bowl.

they choose. The choice of games to watch continues to grow as new cable systems come into use. Wall-sized screens put the viewer in the middle of the action.

Coaches dream of the day when players can practice in a virtual reality simulator similar to those used by airline pilots for flight training. A player could practice a play without involving his teammates and risking injury. His virtual reality helmet would give him the feeling of being on the field . . . and getting smashed by a Reggie White, without the pain.

The greatest changes could come in uniforms and equipment. Players might discuss plays with teammates and coaches through radios in their helmets instead of huddles. Players may have visors instead of face masks and receive written instructions on the visors, transmitted from coaches.

Future uniforms may resemble the one-piece body suits worn by speed skaters. The uniform would be so tight it would appear to be painted on the player, thus eliminating that old standby for making a tackle—grabbing the jersey. Helmets and shoulder pads will be lighter and stronger; one day they may become one unit, giving the neck more protection without hindering the player's range of motion.

Stadiums are being planned with retractable domes and video monitors at every seat for replays and fans' interaction.

Over the final 20 years of the 20th century, there were four major changes in strategy: on offense, the run-and-shoot and West Coast formations; and on defense, the 4–6 alignment and the zone blitz. In some cases, teams reverted to old, long-discarded strategies like the I-formation.

In the early 1980s, field goals accounted for 75 percent of scoring. By the late 1990s, it was 80 percent. In one 1996 game, the Green Bay Packers stopped the Dallas Cowboys seven times inside the Packers' 20-yard line. But

Dallas kicker Chris Boniol kicked seven field goals for a 21–6 victory.

Talks began in the mid-1990s to find ways to reduce the influence of the kicking game. Suggestions included narrowing the goal posts and creating a scoring system based on the distance of the field goal. A field goal inside the 20 might be worth two points, one outside the 50 four points. This kind of scoring system had been debated since the 1890s.

On the field, two of the game's brightest new stars clashed in the 1997 Super Bowl. Curtis Martin, 1995 rookie of the year, showed promise of being the next Emmitt Smith when he rushed for more than 1,000 yards in each of his first two seasons. Martin and quarterback Drew Bledsoe led the New England Patriots into the Super Bowl, where they lost to the Green Bay Packers, whose quarterback, Brett Favre, had been the league's 1995 MVP. Favre is the fourth passer to throw two or more touchdowns in 12 consecutive games. In his first four years, he passed for 108 TDs and had a chance to top Dan Marino in the record books. But the average NFL career is just $4\frac{1}{2}$ years. Favre was just one bad injury from having his career ended.

The NFL had always been slower to expand than other major sports. After admitting Tampa Bay and Seattle into the league in 1976, they waited 19 years before adding Jacksonville and Carolina in 1995. But the success of both teams, who made it to the playoffs in their second season, and the vacating of Cleveland when the Browns moved to Baltimore and became the Ravens in 1996, made it likely that the expansion pace would quicken.

The NFL looked abroad for additional markets. With more worldwide television exposure and exhibition games in cities like London; Tokyo; and Frankfurt, Germany, the NFL created football hotbeds in Europe, Canada, Mexico, and Asia. One day the Super Bowl may be played like soccer's World Cup, where the winners from each country meet to decide a true world champion.

Is all this futuristic talk far-fetched?

Maybe. But there's no disputing that today's NFL is quite different from that first meeting of pro football owners at Hay's Hupmobile Showroom in 1920.

Even without open fields and organized leagues, boys have always found a place to play a pick-up game.

CHRONOLOGY

1874 Harvard and McGill play the first "American football" game.

1880 Walter Camp introduces the line of scrimmage, where players line up on each side of the ball.

1892 On November 13, Pudge Heffelfinger of Yale secretly accepts $500 and $25 expenses to play for the Allegheny Athletic Association, becoming the first paid player.

1920 Representatives of 10 teams meet in Canton, Ohio, and form the American Professional Football Association.

1922 The APFA changes its name to the National Football League.

1929 On November 6, the Chicago Cardinals defeat the Providence Steam Rollers, 16–0, in the first night game.

1932 The Chicago Bears defeat the Portsmouth Spartans, 9–0, for the NFL Championship in the first indoor game. Snow and extreme cold force the game inside Chicago Stadium, where an 80-yard field is created from dirt left over from a circus.

1933 The Boston Redskins introduce the first halftime marching band.

1939 Skip Walz announces the first televised football game, between the Brooklyn Dodgers and Philadelphia Eagles, on October 22.

1960 The American Football League is formed as competition to the NFL.

1963 The Pro Football Hall of Fame opens in Canton, Ohio.

1967 The first Super Bowl is won by the NFL champion Green Bay Packers over the AFL champion Kansas City Chiefs, 35–10.

1970 The AFL and NFL merge.

RULE CHANGES

1880   Walter Camp of Yale creates the line of scrimmage.

1882   Teams have three downs to gain five yards or lose 10, or lose possession.

1883   A scoring system is introduced: 1 point for a safety, 2 for a touchdown, 4 for a goal following a touchdown, and 5 for a goal from the field.

1906   The forward pass is legalized with restrictions.

1912   Teams have four downs to make 10 yards; present scoring system introduced.

1933   Unrestricted passing is legalized.

1938   Roughing the passer becomes a penalty.

1941   Overtime adopted for division playoffs and championships.

1943   Free substitution allowed.

1944   Coaching from the bench allowed.

1955   Ball carrier can no longer get up and run after being knocked down.

1979   Play is dead when quarterback is in grasp of defender.

1986   Instant replay is implemented (and dropped in 1992).

FURTHER READING

Carroll, Bob. *Jim Brown*. New York: Chelsea House, 1992.

Carroll, Bob. *When the Grass Was Real*. New York: Simon & Schuster, 1993.

Hickock, Ralph. *The Pro Football Fan's Companion*. New York: Macmillan, 1995.

Petersen, Robert W. *Pigskin*. New York: Oxford, 1997.

Smith, Byron. *The Pro Football Bio-Bibliography*. West Cornwall, CT: Locust Hill Press, 1989.

Whittingham, Richard. *What a Game They Played*. New York: Harper & Row, 1984.

DENNIS R. TUTTLE, a native of Walnut Cove, N.C., began his sportswriting career at age 17 at his hometown paper, the *Winston-Salem Journal*, in 1977. He has also been a writer and editor at the *Cincinnati Enquirer, Austin American-Statesman, Knoxville Journal*, and *Washington Times*. A 1982 graduate of the University of Cincinnati, he is a two-time winner of an Associated Press Sports Editor's Award for sportswriting excellence. His work has appeared in *The Sporting News, USA Today Baseball Weekly, Baseball America, Inside Sports, Washingtonian,* and *Tuff Stuff* magazines. He authored *Juan Gonzalez* for Chelsea House in 1995, *Albert Belle* in 1997, and *The Composite Guide to Basketball* in 1998. He resides in Cheverly, Maryland.

INDEX